COME GO WITH ME

Howard Thurman and a
Gospel of Radical Inclusivity

C. Anthony Hunt

Come Go With Me
Howard Thurman and a Gospel of Radical Inclusivity
by C. Anthony Hunt

The Rhodes-Fulbright Library series
ALL RIGHTS RESERVED.

ISBN: 978-1-55605-475-4
Ebook: 978-1-55605-476-1

Cover Design by: Kristen E. Hunt

WYNDHAM HALL PRESS
www.wyndhamhallpress.com

Printed in The United States of America

INTRODUCTION

Although I had cursory contact with the writings of Howard Thurman as a seminarian at Wesley Theological Seminary in the early 1990's, and had heard a bit more about him through one of my pastors and mentors, Rev. Dr. Calvin S. Morris, my first substantive engagement with Thurman's life and work was while doing post-graduate and doctoral work in Spiritual Theology at St. Mary's Seminary and University in the mid-1990's. In her class on Spiritual Disciplines (one of the most challenging courses I ever took), Sr. Rose Mary Dougherty introduced our class to Thurman in a way that I had not encountered another pastor, theologian or philosopher. Throughout that semester, I realized that Howard Thurman was the theological voice for which I had been searching. His was a voice that, for me, joined the two often disjoined - "head and heart", spoke to the deep yearnings of the human spirit, and clearly placed Jesus of Nazareth within the context of black struggle, suffering, oppression and overcoming, which was innate to my personal faith and life experience. Through Sr. Dougherty, I found in Thurman - to borrow the sentiments of constructive theologian Dwight Hopkins - theological and spiritual "shoes that fit my feet".

Howard Thurman is considered by many to have been one of the seminal American religious figures of the 20th century. Recognized in 1953 by *Life Magazine* as one of the twelve greatest preachers in America, Thurman has variously been described as a pastor, theologian, philosopher, mystic and prophet. Throughout his ministry, he sought to draw upon the raw materials of life as critical sources of Christian faith in ways that would address his overarching theological concern for the conception, articulation and appropriation of a Christian witness that would give impetus to personal spiritual growth, while ultimately actualizing social transformation, authentic community, and what is argued herein, a gospel of radical inclusivity.

Thurman's work speaks to the perennial concern of persons across denominations and faith traditions as to how to live from a spiritual center, and to integrate matters of the "head and heart", with an impetus towards radically inclusive community.

This volume will examine Howard Thurman's life, ministry and writings in light of the concern of how radically inclusive community might be conceived, articulated and appropriated for the church and society today and in the future. It is proposed that Thurman's Christology - and specifically the explication of the identity of Jesus of Nazareth in his work - was foundational to Thurman's overall theological project, and ultimately served as the framework for his conception of the ministry and mission of the Christian church, and hope for the world.

One does not write outside the context of experience and community, and I am thus indebted to many in my community who have helped shape the thinking that underlies what's written in this volume. As always, I owe debts of gratitude to my family – my wife Lisa, and our children Marcus (deceased), Kristen and Brian. I am thankful for my parents, William Delaney and Amelia Mae Hunt (deceased) who were my first and greatest teachers as to the importance of inclusivity and community. I dedicate this volume to our late son, Marcus William Hunt, who throughout his life embodied what it means to live radically inclusive community. I thank our daughter, Kristen for the cover design for this volume.

I am grateful for the faith community that I have been privileged to lead and serve as pastor since 2011, Epworth Chapel United Methodist Church in Baltimore, Maryland. Daily, we seek to become the radically inclusive community that God calls us to be. For the places where I am privileged to teach, St. Mary's Seminary in University (Baltimore, MD), Wesley Theological Seminary (Washington, DC), United Theological Seminary (Dayton, OH), and the Graduate Theological Foundation (Mishawaka, IN) – I am forever appreciative for the lessons that I've learned and taught about community, and continue to learn.

My prayer is that this volume will serve as a testament to the life and seminal contributions of Rev. Howard Thurman, and speak to our collective hopes as we continue to strive to be radically inclusive community in the days ahead.

CHAPTER ONE

THE MAKING OF A MYSTIC-PROPHET - THE SPIRITUAL AND INTELLECTUAL DEVELOPMENT OF HOWARD THURMAN

"The movement of the Spirit of God in the hearts of men and women often calls them to act against the spirit of their times or causes them to anticipate a spirit which is yet in the making. In a moment of dedication, they are given wisdom and courage to dare a deed that challenges and to kindle a hope that inspires." – Howard Thurman.

Howard Thurman's Early Development and Identity

Born in Daytona Beach, Florida on November 18, 1899, into a climate of segregation and rampant racism, pivotal events of Howard Thurman's young life would serve to shape both his spiritual and intellectual development. The grandson of slaves, Thurman stayed in Daytona Beach until the absence of educational opportunities for Negroes forced him to go to Jacksonville, Florida for a high school education.

At the age of seven, he experienced a profoundly tragic encounter with the Christian church in the aftermath of his father's death. Thurman described his father as a good man who did not identify with the local church. As a result, upon his death, he was viewed by the pastor of that church as one who had died "out of Christ", and, subsequently was refused burial from that church. Thurman's grandmother appealed to the deacons of the church to have the funeral held there and succeeded, however, a traveling evangelist would be the one to conduct the funeral. In Thurman's words, he "preached my father into hell." This would be Thurman's early affirmation that Christianity and the religion of Jesus were not necessarily one and the same.[1]

In ensuing years, Thurman found solace and strength of purpose in communing with nature. An oak tree, for instance, became his refuge as he leaned back against the strong trunk experiencing the strength of its high branches which bent with the wind but did not break. These were formative experiences in the development of Thurman's spiritual perspectives. His baptism at the age of twelve, marking his acceptance as a member of the church, instilled a sense of personal identity as he shared ownership in a community of God's people. His grandmother, Nancy Ambrose, was instrumental in his development as a member of the community of faith.[2]

Thurman's education in the public-school system of Daytona Beach presented formidable challenges. There were no educational opportunities for black children after completing the seventh grade. The reasoning of the public-school system was simple, although tragic in consequence. If there were no black children completing the eighth grade, there would be no need for a black high school. Thurman, however, was fortunate in having his elementary school principal teach him individually, resulting in his successful completion of the eighth grade and the addition of an eighth-grade level to the Negro public school shortly after.[3] His education continued as he attended high school in Jacksonville beginning with the aid of a kind gentleman at the Daytona train station who paid the freight charge for his steamer trunk. These acts of kindness would be remembered by Thurman as instrumental episodes in the development of his spiritual life. He would go on to complete his undergraduate studies at Morehouse College in Atlanta, Georgia (1923), and his graduate studies in theology at the Rochester Divinity School in Rochester, New York (1926). Thurman's ministerial career formally began in Oberlin, Ohio where, from 1926 until 1928, he pastored an African-American Baptist congregation. From 1932-44, he served as Dean of Andrew Rankin Memorial Chapel and Professor of Theology at Howard University. Prominent among his many involvements, however, was the San Francisco-based church which he co-founded and co-pastored with Rev. Dr. Alfred Fisk from 1944-53 – The Church for the Fellowship of All Peoples (Fellowship Church) – heralded as the first authentically inclusive, multicultural model of institutional religion in the United States. In 1953, Thurman became the first African-American dean at a majority white university, as the Dean of Marsh Chapel and Professor of Spiritual Resources and Disciplines at Boston University. During this same period, he formed the Howard Thurman Educational Trust, which disburses funds for various humanitarian endeavors, most notably scholarships for African-American students in the South.[4]

Howard Thurman was a multidimensional person who sought to live fully on all levels of existence – physical, intellectual, emotional and spiritual. Describing his attributes is like constructing a bridge. The bridge, to be effective, must reach both sides, or the traveler will fall.[5] Vincent Harding captured the essence of Thurman as a "God-intoxicated" man when he wrote about Thurman in the introduction to *For the Inward Journey*. Harding observed that Thurman was a person who was constantly moving towards the source of all human life and truth via the concrete beauty and terror of the black experience in the United States.[6]

Spiritual and Intellectual Influences

In assessing Howard Thurman's intellectual development, Mozella G. Mitchell makes the important observation that "for one reason or another ... perhaps for many reasons, one no doubt being the social limitations he faced as a Black American, Thurman chose a route of development different from the systematic. He chose to remain free of the restrictions of any exact discipline such as literature, theology, psychology, or philosophy.[7] Thurman never altered his ideas to conform either to the standard university or ecclesiastical life.

In his seminal work, *Howard Thurman: The Mystic as Prophet,* Luther E. Smith places Thurman's life within the context of the dual attributes of his mystical nature and prophetic witness.[8] Smith suggests that four persons stand out as having had a crucial impact upon the development of Thurman's thought and spirituality: Nancy Ambrose, George Cross, Henry B. Robins, and Rufus Jones.[9] These persons would serve as the major influencers for Thurman intellectually, as well as spiritually, and would help to shape his philosophy and practice of community-building.

A. *Nancy Ambrose*

While scholars like Cross, Robins and Jones significantly impacted Howard Thurman intellectually and spiritually in his later life, it was his maternal grandmother, Nancy Ambrose who cultivated his spirit and mind from an early age. Of his grandmother, Thurman said:

> I learned more, for instance, about the genius of the religion of Jesus from my grandmother than from all the men who taught me all ... the Greek and the rest of it.

Because she moved inside the experience and lived out of that kind of center…[10]

Reared by his beloved Grandma Nancy, a former slave, young Thurman regularly read the Bible aloud to her as a child. From her, he learned not only of the trials of slavery, but also of the slaves' deep religious faith, which profoundly shaped his vision of the transformative promise of Christianity. Nancy Ambrose appropriated a "religious essence" that was not just in dialogue with concern for the world but with the particular issue of what it means to be black in America. Thurman was profoundly influenced by his grandmother's views on religion and racism. Much of her thinking is captured in her views of Scripture. Thurman wrote:

Two or three times a week I read the Bible aloud to her. I was deeply impressed by the fact that she was most particular about the choice of Scripture. For instance, I might read many of the more devotional Psalms, some of Isaiah, the Gospels again and again, but the Pauline epistles, never – except at long intervals, the thirteenth chapter of First Corinthians… With the feeling of great temerity, I asked her one day why it was that she would not let me read any of the Pauline letters. What she told me I shall never forget. "During the days of slavery," she said, "the master's minister would occasionally hold services for the slaves. Old man McGhee was so mean that he would not let a Negro minister preach to his slaves. Always the white minister used as his text: 'Slaves, be obedient to your master… as unto Christ.' Then he would go on to show how it was God's will that we were slaves and how, if we were good and happy slaves, God would bless us. I promised my Maker that

11

if I ever learned to read and if freedom ever came, I would not read that part of the Bible."[11]

In contrast, she often told the story of the black preacher who had a different message for the slaves. In their gathering he would say: "You are not slaves, you are not niggers – you are God's children!" As his grandmother finished her story with those lines, a kind of transformation took place in her. According to Thurman: "she would unconsciously straighten up, head high and chest out, and a faraway look would come on her face."[12]

Throughout his lectures and writings, Thurman spoke of his grandmother in saintly, yet intimate tones. The prominence he gave to her ideas and example can be understood when one considers her meaning in the making of his personality. In a period of Thurman's life when his world seemed wrought with insecurity and death, she had attributes which translated into power. She acted as one who had inner authority. Rather than being controlled by her environment she exercised control over it. Nancy Ambrose became a role model for him. She was the exemplary mentor.[13]

Ambrose was not a scholar *per se,* but a sapient personality who understood the value of a cultivated mind. As a young girl living on a Florida plantation in the ante-bellum period, no prospects for liberty existed, but early on she established the grounds for freedom. Liberty was conferred from without, but freedom, she discovered, was founded from within. She never received any formal education, yet she was acutely aware of its importance. When the owner's daughter was punished for trying to teach her the rudiments of reading and counting, Ambrose knew "there must be some magic in knowing how to read and write."[14] Later, she would communicate to her grandson a fundamental reason for obtaining the "magic" of knowledge, sharing this message: "Your only chance is to get an education. The white man will destroy you if you don't."[15]

Ambrose was for Thurman, a source of protection, faith and hope. Elizabeth Yates, a Thurman biographer, described Ambrose's significance in his life as follows:

She backed up her words with action and he knew he could count on her. He boasted to his friends of her, saying she could kill a bear with her fist. No one disputed him, though no one felt a need for a test. There was not a person in the Negro community on the shore of the Halifax River who had not at a time of trouble felt anchored by her strength. She was a haven to them all. More than anyone else, she made Howard feel his significance, not only as a Negro boy but as a Child of God.[16]

The profound influence of Nancy Ambrose on Thurman and his understanding of Christian love, nonviolence and radically inclusive community is evident in a story from his childhood. After fighting another boy, he went home bruised and tattered. As he faced his grandmother, the following exchange took place:

"No one ever wins a fight," were her only words as she looked at me. "But I beat him," I said. "Yes, but look at you. You beat him, but you will learn someday that nobody ever wins a fight." [17]

It is not difficult to see the influence of Ambrose in Thurman's stress that the individual, rather than the institution or the group, is the key to social change. She was an individual who survived personal tragedy, challenged the church, influenced the local community, found integrity and worth in her racial identity, fearlessly confronted any aggressive action from their hostile environment, and who drew upon personal religious experience as the source of her life.[18]

Nancy Ambrose's influence on Thurman proves that we are more than just the product of our environment and certainly we do not have to be the victim of it, but we can become bigger than it and change agents within it.

B. George Cross

George Cross taught Howard Thurman systematic theology during Thurman's last year and a half of seminary education at Rochester Divinity School (1925-1926). Cross's influence on Thurman can be seen first in Cross's pursuit of an element which he identified as the *essence* of the Christian faith. This *essence* is the basic, unchanging, unifying truth that characterizes and genuinely manifests the faith. It may be found in Christian doctrines, dogmas, creeds, and theologies, but it is never fully contained in them. This *essence* has the fundamental qualities common to all religions, yet it is distinctive within Christianity, according to Cross.[19]

The essence of Christianity is what Cross endeavored to define through his method for doing apologetics.[20] It is characterized in the following ways:

> *1.* It is "a quality of spiritual life," where one acknowledges that one's ultimate interests and commitments must be with spiritual concerns.
>
> *2.* The personality of Jesus Christ is the basis for understanding the essence. In Jesus, the Christian finds the perfect life. And through spiritual

fellowship with this perfect life, its teachings and the meaning of its example, the Christian finds the way to "the higher life."

3. It has distinctive qualities that are similar to other religions. It takes the individual into a consciousness of the relation to God, which brings fulfillment to the heart like no other religion. Other religions are "Christianity in its beginning or lower stages."[21]

4. It is the practice of the most perfect fellowship, where the potentialities in every person are appreciated, developed and made available to the needs of others.

5. It is "one and the same with true morality." Love and devotion to God mean love and devotion to the welfare of our fellow man and woman.

6. It has the power for moral redemption, such that it delivers humanity from the domination of evil.

7. It creates the experience of perfect peace for the believer. In the midst of suffering, fear and anxieties, this essence gives confidence and power to withstand and overcome.

The telos of George Cross's conception of Christian essence is to lead the individual and community to salvation. In his book, *Christian Salvation,* Cross defined salvation this way:

...to the modern Protestant it is the bringing of the man into such a fellowship with God as gives him a self-mastery and a self-devotion to the highest end of life. It is the entrance into an experience of conscious unity of life with one's fellowmen, a participation in the ministry of a universal good. It is to be endowed with that spirit of enterprise that enables him to turn the forces of the material world toward their true end, to make them angels of mercy sent forth to do service for the sake of them that shall inherit salvation.[22]

According to Cross, there must be individual salvation before a community can be saved. Christian salvation is ultimately the movement towards "perfect community" or "shalom." Perfect community for Cross is actualized at the place and time where persons are able to exercise their full potential and be in loving relationship with other individuals.

Thurman's major disagreement with the liberalism espoused by Cross was the fatuous positivism it displayed. Modernism's unmitigated belief in national destiny and world progress served to obscure the malignancy and pervasiveness of domestic evils, particularly as regards racism. For Thurman, a theological stance so readily given to ignoring hostilities directed at vast segments of the population (African Americans, women, various immigrant groups, etc.) was itself seriously impaired. He understood such optimism to be a critical, if not fatal, departure from social reality, utterly irreconcilable with his own experience as one of the dominated and disinherited.

Despite Thurman's attestation that Cross was the teacher who had a "greater influence on my mind than any other person who ever lived," Thurman remained at variance with the idea of leisurely introspection as the means to human attainment. He shared deeply in the concern of Cross and Henry B. Robins for the centrality of human personality, the universal life of the spirit, and other liberal motifs, but he had to express the "hunger of the spirit" which they encouraged, inclusive of his own racial fact.[23]

C. Henry B. Robins

Henry B. Robins was professor of Religious Education and the History and Philosophy of Religion and Missions at Rochester Divinity School while Howard Thurman was a student there. Robins is credited with identifying for Thurman the *religious essence*, which is found in all expressions of religion. While George Cross's essence is the cohesive factor for Christian Apologetics, Robin's essence is the cohesiveness in Comparative Religion. For both Cross and Robins, Christianity is the culmination of the evolutionary process. Christianity, at its core, is universal in character. It has the ability to include and speak meaningfully to the religious aspirations of all the world's peoples. This universal quality makes it the greatest missionary religion.[24]

For Robins, the purpose of the essence is the "Kingdom of God," while Cross viewed purpose in the context of the "saved community." The Kingdom of God is the perfect human fellowship where redemptive love is fulfilled.[25]

While Cross was the one who commissioned Thurman to garner all his energies to address the "hunger of the spirit," Thurman credited Robins as the teacher who "was as close to introducing me (Thurman) to the life of the spirit as any professor I had."[26] Cross raised the importance of spiritual matters. Robins gave definition to them, particularly their unifying and universal qualities. But most importantly, Robins led Thurman to an understanding of how he (Thurman) was to participate in the "spiritual adventure."

D. Rufus Jones

The liberal reconstruction of religion and the concern for social disorganization that emerged in the late nineteenth century was the inheritance of Rufus Jones. This orientation,

17

combined with Jones's deep roots in the mystical tradition of Quakerism, formed the framework for his thought. Thurman credited Jones along with George Cross as having most prominently "opened the way in my thinking." [27] Jones's consuming interest in life was to interpret the validity of the mystical experience and the social role of the mystic. He was one of three leading interpreters of mysticism during his time, William James and Evelyn Underhill being the others. Jones rejected James's psychological emphasis, and Underhill's near obsession with the substantive dimensions of mystical experience, as important as this was, for a more deliberate functional analysis.[28]

Thurman became aware of Jones through his book, *Finding the Trail of Life.* Upon finishing the book, Thurman had a feeling of "instant kinship" with the author. He initiated correspondence with Jones, and for six months during 1929 became a "special student of Philosophy" in residence with this Quaker mystic at Haverford College.[29]

Jones gave Thurman his first extensive exposure to the historical, philosophical and experiential dimensions of mysticism. Though Thurman had remembered experiences of mystical consciousness since childhood, the internship brought definition, discipline, and perspective to the experiences. Jones boldly underscored Robin's emphasis that religion is to be an experience. More than any other teacher, Jones formed the nexus that religious experience, at its profoundest level, is mystical experience.

Jones, was deeply committed to a theology which claims issues of justice, freedom and peace as inherent interests of the religious venture. Commitment to the spiritual life is a commitment to that power which is able to save the world.

Spiritual issues are the very ground of all material concerns (e.g., politics, civil rights, poverty, violence, etc.).

Specifically, it was Jones who offered a linkage that gave Thurman the vision of how spiritual power could address the conditions that oppressed him as a black person in America. Thurman confirmed the significance of this linkage when he wrote:

> ...all my life I have been seeking to validate, beyond all ambivalence and frustrations, the integrity of the inner life... I have sought a way of life that could come under the influence of, and be informed by, the fruits of the inner life. The cruel vicissitudes of the social situation in which I have been forced to live in American society have made it vital for me to seek resources, or a resource, to which I could have access as I sought means for sustaining the personal enterprise of my life beyond all the ravages inflicted upon it by the brutalities of the social order.[30]

According to Jones, the problem of race could be forcefully addressed through the ministry of the Spirit. Or more specifically, the race question could be understood as a spiritual matter.

In the final analysis, none of us are really self-made – our *Sitz im Leben* (worldview) is shaped by multifarious sets of people and experiences, and that was the case with Howard Thurman. He was shaped by (1) his rearing the American South, with its distinctive ethos, (2) his familial upbringing – especially the impact of his grandmother, Nancy Ambrose, (3) the religious and social teachings of the Black Baptist church, and (4) the patterns of racial segregation that he observed and experienced in the South. Intellectuals like George Cross,

Henry Robins and Rufus Jones played significant roles in Thurman's further development. Each of them brought something distinctive to Thurman's views and thoughts. Cross brought to Thurman the challenge to address the essence of religion, and "the hunger of the spirit"; Robins introduced him to, "the life of the Spirit"; and Jones offered Thurman an entrée into the life of mysticism. These three dimensions, again, helped to shape a *Sitz im Leben* and a philosophy of ministry that impacted Thurman's life, and impacted the church and world in and through his ministry.

E. Evangelical Liberalism

It has been suggested that the theological perspectives of Howard Thurman generally fall within the tradition of evangelical liberalism. Kenneth Cauthen in his book, *The Impact of American Religious Liberalism* defines the tradition in the following way:

> The [evangelical liberals] stood squarely within the Christian traditions and accepted as normative for their thinking what they understood to be the *essence* of historical Christianity. The men had a deep consciousness of their continuity with the mail line of Christian orthodoxy and felt that they were preserving its *essential* features in terms that were suitable to the modern world. One of the evidences of the loyalty of the evangelical liberals to the historic faith is the place that they give to Jesus. Through his person and work there is mediated to men both knowledge of God and saving power. He is the source and norm of the Christian's experience of God. In short, evangelical liberalism is Christocentric.[31]

The essence of evangelical liberalism affirms a religious teleology in which Christianity wins the world to profess Jesus Christ as Lord. The saved community is the Christian community. The Kingdom of God is more precisely the Kingdom of God in Christ. Christianity's goal is to convert individuals and societies to "the way" of Jesus; any achievement less than this is inadequate.[32]

Thurman placed a high value on the human personality, regarding personality as a reflection of the soul and therefore an image of the divine. The personality is not only an expression of the soul's individuality; it is a unique image of God. Because every personality is divine in essence, every personality is endowed with dignity and worth. Thurman focused on the nature of the person as the central focus of religion in the context of community-building. He proposed that spiritual impoverishment, deriving from an improper sense of self, was the fundamental cause of moral decay in society. Where individuals have a proper sense of self, the stage is set for strong moral forces to shape a moral and secure society.

This reasoning faced sharp criticism from Reinhold Niebuhr who continually spoke about the defects in Christian liberalism. Niebuhr, in *Moral Man and Immoral Society,* argued that the ethical considerations which govern relations between individuals are not the same as those which govern inter-group relations. One may be willing to make all kinds of personal sacrifices to live the ethical life (moral man), but the same sacrifice may be too much to expect of a body politic (immoral society). As an individual, one may have the right to face emaciating and abusive conditions as a symbol of protest against politics, but the same individual may decide that a more violent response is required if those conditions threaten his/her fellows. A group is not just the sum total of its individual members. A group can have a consciousness and value system which differs from those of individual members.[33]

When this problem was posed to Thurman, he admitted the difficulties that arose in his moral position. He stated that while he might be certain about a nonviolent response to an act of violence perpetrated against him, he might react differently if his wife were in the same danger.[34] Niebuhr's thesis raised serious dilemmas for Thurman's focus on the ethical individual as the key to the ethical society. The ethical individual may be very responsible in interpersonal relations, and be ill-prepared to be the ethical social or political leader of other decision-makers for society.

In contrast to Thurman's conception of the Christian love-ethic, Niebuhr believed life must not only be governed by a concept of love, but also by a distinct and profound concept of justice.[35] It is necessary for love to be accompanied by justice. Niebuhr's perspective is in concert with the assertion of Martin Luther King, Jr. that "true peace is not merely the absence of tension, it is the presence of justice." King agreed with Niebuhr that justice could be a fulfillment of love. Niebuhr said, "Yet the law of love is involved in all approximations of justice, not only as the source of the norms of justice, but as an ultimate perspective by which their limitations are discovered."[36]

Yet, Thurman maintained that the movement from the inner experience of community within the self is the basis for social transformation. His understanding of the movement from the "inner" to the "outer" dimensions of religious experience has profound implications for spirituality and social change, and serves as a corrective to the tendency of one-dimensional theological discourse that exalts the social dynamics of community at the expense of the individual relationship between God and the self. Mozella Gordon Mitchell posits that

Thurman's contribution to black theology rests on his provision of an intellectual framework for a proper *sense of self* and *urge toward community*.[37] Walter E. Fluker posits that Thurman's shamanistic endeavor to lead the individual to the inner resources of being, which he described as "the hunger of the heart," is a cogent reminder that the work for harmony and wholeness in the world cannot be accomplished without the cultivation of the inner life.[38]

Thurman and the Vocation of a Mystic-Prophet

Historian Lerone Bennett, Jr. in his eulogy of Howard Thurman in 1981, pointed to Thurman's perspective on life, "A man cannot be at home everywhere, unless he is at home somewhere."[39] One has to know from whence they have come in order to understand how they are to operate within the context of present reality and future possibility. Thurman seemed to be at home with his roots in Southern black culture, and yet was able to practice ministry in ways that transcended cultural and theological perspectives.

Several scholars have asserted that Thurman's primary identity was that of a mystic.[40] Briefly defined, the mystic is one who believes that she or he has experienced a special angle of perception or encounter with ultimacy (however construed), which encounter departs from normative social constructions of what is "real."[41] Cheslyn Jones of Oxford University suggested that there seem to be four constants in mystical experience. First, the mystic is in touch with an 'object' which is invisible, intangible and inaccessible, beyond sensual contact. Second, the 'object' is inexhaustible, infinite and incomprehensible (in the present sense it cannot be captured or surrounded), and therefore is also inexpressible, beyond full description. Third, the contact is intuitive, 'immediate' (unmediated) and direct, even if after introduction by a third party or book. Fourth, even so, there is an inward affinity between the 'object' and the person, an attraction or fascination, even leading to mutual interpenetration or communion.[42]

For Thurman, the construct that best characterizes his spiritual theology, as referenced by the likes of Cheslyn Jones, is Thurman's practice of mysticism – more simply characterized as unmediated encounter with the divine (God). This can be seen in the "caughtness" of Thurman's practice of theology. There are essentially four dimensions of Thurman's mystical practice of spirituality (or spiritual theology) – Thurman's view of: (1) God, (2) himself, (3) nature, and (4) life. This is the making of a substantive spiritual theology/spirituality, and what became, according to Luther Smith, of Thurman's identity as essentially a "mystic-prophet".

Thurman's search for community is intricately connected to the yearning for an irreducible essence as rooted in his own search for a Christ-centered spirituality and sense of personal encounter and connectedness with God. This yearning for God-connectedness is evident in Thurman's prayer:

> Lord, I want to be more holy in my heart.
> Here is the citadel of all my desiring,
> where my hopes are born,
> and all the deep resolutions of my spirit take wings.
> In this center, my fears are nourished,
> and all my hates are nurtured.
> Here my loves are cherished,
> all the deep hungers of my spirit are honored
> without quivering and without shock.
> In my heart, above all else,
> let love and integrity envelop me

until my love is perfected and the last vestige
of my desiring is no longer in conflict with thy Spirit.
Lord, I want to be more holy in my heart.[43]

Thurman's desire to encounter and experience God is
further articulated in another of his prayers:

O Holy God,
open to me
light for my darkness,
courage for my fear,
hope for my despair.
O loving God,
open for me
wisdom for my confusion,
forgiveness for my sins,
love for my hate.
O God of peace,
open for me
peace for my turmoil,
joy for my sorrow,
strength for my weakness.
O generous God,
open my heart
to receive all your gifts.

In his life and work, Thurman sought to "utilize the raw
materials of daily experience as the time and place for
encountering God.[44] He viewed nature as critical to helping
persons understand the life of the spirit. At one point he
compared life to a river. The river flows, constantly seeking to
connect with its source – the sea. In human life, persons
perpetually seek to discover that which is the source of life – the

source of being and the source of meaning. That being the divine source.[45]

In his reflection, "The Will to Live," Thurman described a personal encounter with nature that helped him experience existence at a deeper level. He wrote:

> You have seen trees growing out of sheer rock; or roots, finding no soil below or being unable to penetrate the rocky substance of the earth, spread themselves, fan shape, on the surface, sending their tendrils into every crevice and cranny where hidden moisture and soil fragments accumulate. You have seen human beings with their bodies reduced to mere skeletons and all the vestiges of health wiped out – yet for interminable periods they continue breathing, as if to breathe were life.[46]

While walking down a street in Georgia, Thurman recounted the story of having observed a tree that had broken through the concrete pavement. The pavement could not contain the tree's desire to live. In spreading itself and breaking through, the tree demonstrated its determination to live.

Thurman's yearning for the fullness of life, and for an appropriation of radically inclusive community was rooted in his own spirituality. In *Meditations of the Heart,* he wrote:

> Here is in every person an inward sea, and in that sea there is an island and on that island there is an altar, and standing before that altar is the "angel with the flaming sword." Nothing can get by that angel to be placed upon that altar unless it has the mark of the inner authority. Nothing passes "the angel with the flaming sword" to be placed upon your altar unless it is a part of "the fluid of your consent." This is your crucial link to the Eternal.[47]

Thurman's intense belief in the importance of personal, private experience with God has resulted in his being labeled an advocate of personal piety. This labeling is not completely accurate, according to Luther Smith.[48] Although Thurman's insistence on self-awareness and transformation can be cast within the pietistic tradition, he had just as intense a commitment to community. His mystical experiences were the basis of this commitment to community. Thurman wrote:

> It is in the moment of [mystical] vision that there is a sense of community – a unity not only with God, but a unity with all of life, particularly with human life. It is in the moment of vision that the mystic discovers that (their) "private values are undergirded and determined by a structure which far transcends the limits of one's individual self."…The ascetic impulse having as its purpose individual purification and living brings the realistic mystic face to face with the society in which he functions as a person. He discovers that his is a person and a personality [which] in a profound sense can only be achieved in a milieu of human relations. Personality is something more than mere individuality – it is a fulfillment of the logic of individuality in community.[49]

Thurman was a mystic who recognized the necessity of social activism for enabling and responding to religious experience. This is evident in his assertion:

> Therefore, the mystic's concern with the imperative of social action is not merely to improve the condition of society. It is not merely to feed the hungry, not merely to relieve human suffering and human misery. If this were all, in and of itself, it would be important surely.

But this is not all. The basic consideration has to do with the removal of all that prevents God from coming to himself in the life of the individual. Whatever there is that blocks this, calls for action.[50]

He argued that pure asceticism is limited in that it in itself typically does not lead to conscious social action. Here, we begin to see the interconnection of mysticism with prophetic witness in Thurman's thought and praxis. In Segundo Galilea's article "Liberation as an Encounter with Politics and Contemplation," there is confirmation for Thurman's convictions about the process of moving from the autonomy of the mystic to the prophetic unity of community. [51] Galilea writes:

> Authentic Christian contemplation, passing through the desert, transforms contemplatives into prophets and heroes of commitment and militants into mystics. Christianity achieves the synthesis of the politician and the mystic, the militant and the contemplative, and abolishes the false antithesis between the religious-contemplative and the militantly committed. Authentic contemplation, through the encounter with the absolute of God, leads to the absolute of one's neighbor.[52]

Galilea then describes effective responses to contemplation, which make a better world (community). One response is political activity, which involves the contemplative in party politics. A second response, which describes Thurman's commitments and ministry, is what Galilea calls "the prophetic pastoral option." He characterizes the option in the following way:

In it [the prophetic pastoral option] charity, the source of contemplation, is channeled into the effective proclamation of the message of Christ about the liberation of the poor and the "least." The message becomes a *critical consciousness*, and is capable of inspiring the deepest and most decisive liberating transformation. In this sense it has social and political consequences. [53]

In his work, *Mysticism and Social Change*, Alton B. Pollard argues that Thurman appropriated a construct, "affirmation mysticism" where our God encounters may lead to concrete social action.[54] Pollard employs the phrase "mystic-activism" as a description of Thurman's involvements. Thurman's was a form of mysticism – rooted in historic cenobitic monastic perspective - which sought to constructively engage in the process of community-building. A designation of Thurman within the context of mystic-activism focuses attention on the real potential of mysticism as a discomforting yet compelling call to action.[55]

Mystic-activism is a praxis-orientation to the world that relies – at least in part – on the political and intellectual arguments and dictates of society. [56] For Thurman, transformed individuals are the first step in the remaking of the social order into a peaceful and just society. True community can only be established when transformed individuals act within and upon social structures, and become involved in social mechanisms. The movement toward radically inclusive community through social action (demonstrations, running for public office, critiquing social institutions and structures, community organizing and boycotts) is a natural consequence of personal piety.

Thurman's constant yearning was to move towards a clearer personal and communal comprehension of what he often referred to as "the irreducible essence" of life. Activist Jesse L. Jackson recounts how Thurman would often challenge him to move toward this "irreducible essence." According to Jackson, Thurman insisted that if you ever developed a cultivated will, with spiritual discipline, the striving for community would persist. The irreducible essence, developed through the cultivated will with spiritual discipline, would result in spiritual and social transformation.[57]

Alton Pollard further offers the concept "social regeneration" as the type of mystical action in which Thurman engaged. Social regeneration discloses an ethical program working on three levels – synchronizing intra-individual (personal), inter-individual (communal) and inter-group (societal) orderliness. In Thurman's case, social regeneration denotes a holistic process that is generally critical of church and society, but not in a fundamentally hostile or negating sense. The impetus for social regeneration lies not so much in social structures as in the transformation of individuals, who alone are capable of generating a force fully vibrant and sufficient to break through oppressive structures. Social regeneration is increasingly effected as enough individuals experience the transforming "sense of wholeness" or ethical orderliness, and the will to implement its verity in society. The aim of social regeneration is not to perpetuate conflict in society simply because or whenever there is no abiding evidence of hope, but in order to facilitate and increase rapprochement between individuals and social groupings. This is the *sine qua non* for Thurman's advancement of the concept of "community."[58]

In Thurman's life and ministry, there is evidence that social regeneration can lead to social activism. The unconditional seriousness of the religious experience itself impels social corroboration, causing one to engage "the powers of this world" with a strident social dimension. The knowledge accrued in this encounter is relational and transactional in character, ushering in a personally transformative system of values and a new, or at the very least, revitalized mode of interaction with others (community and society) and God. The impetus for social regeneration occurs when an individual's ultimate allegiances – race, creed, gender, nationality and socio-economic standing are transvalued to a less defensive, penultimate status.[59]

In terms of prophetic thought and praxis, Thurman's ministry can also be clearly viewed within the context of four expressions of the prophetic as explicated by Walter Brueggemann in *The Prophetic Imagination*. Brueggemann posits that four characteristics emerge as indicators of prophetic ministry: (1) the establishment of an "alternative community" which is conscious of its unique identity and mission to others; (2) the prophetic insights are communicated in every activity of ministry, and they define sources of life and death for every context; (3) persons are helped in seeing the world as it really is, and to become fully sensitive to the hurt and pain experienced in life; and (4) prophetic ministry seeks to penetrate despair so that new futures can be believed in and embraced by us.[60]

Luther Smith asserts that when you study a prophet, you simultaneously study his people. The prophet's significance is the result of his relationship with his community.[61] Over the course of his life and ministry, Thurman lived into the divine moral and prophetic imperative that the church and society share in seeking to eradicate racial hatred, economic oppression and social disintegration, and advanced the appropriation of the Christian love-ethic as foundational for constructively moving

31

towards the realization of radically inclusive community. Thurman's prophetic leadership, preaching and praxis offer insight for the contemporary church and its leaders - and has implications and application in at least four principle areas of prophetic witness: ***Call, Conviction, Courage and Commitment.***

1. ***Call*** - During Thurman's almost six decades of public ministry, it became clear that his praxis of ministry in the public sphere was ultimately rooted in a deep sense of a prophetic call by God. This sense of calling is what ultimately spawned his action. Early in his ministry, he came to the conclusion that it was indeed a part of his vocation and calling to become one of the prophetic public voices in the search for common ground in religion and the world, first at Rankin Chapel at Howard University, then at Fellowship Church in San Francisco, and then as Dean at Boston University, and beyond.

2. ***Conviction*** - For Thurman, his sense of calling was acted upon within the context of his convictions. His convictions were largely rooted in his understanding of God and people. He believed that all persons were created by God with inherent worth, and that all people were therefore privy to the moral prerogative of human dignity and social justice. Thurman consistently affirmed what he deemed to be the "essence of being" in all people regardless of race, class or other categories. Ultimately, it was his convictions that led to his prophetic witness.

3. ***Courage*** – For Thurman, courage served as the measure of human will to act on his call and convictions – and to

say and do what he believed to be just and right. St. Augustine of Hippo stated, "Hope has two beautiful daughters; their names are *Anger* and *Courage. Anger* at the way things are, and *Courage* to see that they do not remain as they are." Courage to act on one's call and convictions means one is willing to risk much of oneself - one's popularity, position, promotion and associations for the sake of the causes to which one feels called and convicted to prophetically address. Thurman's sense of courage is evident in his prayer, "Give me courage to live" –

> *Give me the courage to live! Really live– not merely exist.*
> *Live dangerously, Scorning risk!*
> *Live honestly, Daring the truth– particularly the truth of myself!*
> *Live resiliently– Ever changing, ever growing, ever adapting."*

4. **Commitment** - Thurman stated that "Commitment means that it is possible for a man to yield the nerve center of his consent to a purpose or cause, a movement or an ideal, which may be more important to him than whether he lives or dies."[62]   This speaks clearly to Thurman's sense of the critical role of commitment to promoting racial equality and social justice, and his strivings to help articulate and appropriate what would become a form of radically inclusive community. It was out of his sense of calling, conviction and courage that Thurman's commitments to seek community and common ground across human diversity derived.

CHAPTER TWO
MOHANDAS GANDHI, HOWARD THURMAN
AND THE POWER OF LOVE

"Do not be silent; there is no limit to the power that may be released through you." – **Howard Thurman**

The encounters of Howard Thurman with the thinking of Mohandas Gandhi were critical in helping to shape Thurman's understanding and philosophy of nonviolence as an "active force" of resistance. As Sudarshan Kapur pointed out in his book *Raising Up a Prophet: The African-American Encounter with Gandhi*, black intellectuals' encounter with Gandhi, beginning in the 1930s (including Benjamin Mays, William Stuart Nelson, and Edward Carroll) laid the theological foundation that Thurman was able to develop with regard to the Christian love-ethic and radically inclusive community.[63]

Gandhi provided a deep reservoir of ideas from which Thurman drank. Thurman may not have been equipped with the most rigorous understanding of nonviolent principles if not for his exposure to Gandhi, although he had been committed – at least to some degree - to the transforming ideals of nonviolence prior to encountering the thought of Gandhi. His contact with Gandhi would serve to codify his thinking with regard to nonviolence, while also serving as an impetus for his ongoing search for the realization of what Thurman deemed to be "common ground", which would find its ultimate expression in radically inclusive community.

I. Towards a Spirituality and Philosophy of Nonviolence
A. Gandhi's Early Development

Mohandas K. Gandhi was born in India in 1869 into the Vaisa caste (merchants, farmers, and craftspeople).[64] His father, however, was involved in law and politics. His mother was a very religious person. A devout Hindu, she engaged in self-discipline, purification and other religious observances. Gandhi's India was dominated by British colonialism. In Rajkot, he experienced early segregation. The British reserved for themselves the best part of town; Indians were restricted to the slums. At school, he was taught in English, under the assumption that everything Indian was inferior. Gandhi disliked this arrangement. He felt that Indians needed the pride of language, custom and history. With his pride of self and people, Gandhi studied both Sanskrit and Persian.[65]

When he decided to go to England to study law, Gandhi came up against the stark reality of the caste system, and racial and religious disintegration. His family told him that if he crossed the ocean to a foreign land, he would become an outcast. Gandhi, however, did not yield to this threat and vowed to be a Hindu wherever he was. A family priest intervened on his behalf and assured everyone that, if Gandhi kept his vow, he could remain a Hindu. This led Gandhi to declare war against the strictures and harshness of the caste system, and this conviction remained with him for the rest of his life.[66]

In England, Gandhi's philosophy of nonviolence began to take shape. He studied the ideas of Hindus, Buddhists and Christians. He was moved as well by the writings of American authors such as Ralph Waldo Emerson and Henry David

Thoreau. Thoreau's ideas, especially on civil disobedience, impressed Gandhi. His encounter with the New Testament, especially with Jesus and the Sermon on the Mount, also had a profound impact on his thinking.

B. Development of Satyagraha

Faith was the center of life for Gandhi. He believed in God, and in truth. "What I want to achieve, what I have been striving and pining to achieve these thirty years," he wrote in his autobiography, "is self-realization, to see God face to face. I live and move and have my being in pursuit of this goal. All that I do by way of speaking and writing, and all my ventures in the political field, are directed to the same end." Gandhi saw the face of God in the poorest peasant and in the struggle of nonviolent resistance and love in the public realm. He sought to uncover truth at every turn and found that justice and nonviolence spring from the journey in truth. "You may be sent to the gallows, or put to torture, but if you have truth in you, you will experience an inner joy." Truth, for Gandhi, was the essence of life.[67]

The formative ideas of Gandhi's philosophy began to take shape in the years he worked to better the social and economic conditions of Indians in South Africa. Gandhi spent 20 years of his life in South Africa as an acknowledged leader of the Indian people.[68] Rajmohan Gandhi, research professor at the Center of Policy Research, New Delhi, India suggests that much of Gandhi's view on nonviolence can be traced to his personal experiences and early encounters with bigotry on his journey to South Africa in 1893. [69] Rajmohan Gandhi offers an account, depicted in the Attenborough film, of the well-know incident when Mohandas Gandhi was ejected from the railway train at the station of Pietermaritzburg in 1893:

36

The barrister trained in London, he was holding a first-class ticket and had just arrived in South Africa – he had been there hardly a week. Because he did not have the right skin color and did not move to the van compartment when asked, he was thrown out. Then he made a journey by train, coach, and train again, eventually arriving, via Johannesburg. Along the way he was roughly beaten on the coach because he refused to sit as ordered on the floor. He tried to spend the stopover night in Johannesburg in a hotel, but was told that there was no room. He had experiences that were not very pleasant. On a Sunday evening he arrived in Pretoria, his destination. Not sure of what lay ahead of him, and remembering that he could not get accommodations in Johannesburg, he wondered where he would spend his first night in Pretoria. He decided to consult the man who was checking tickets at the exit for ideas. While he was having this conversation, a Black American noticed the predicament of the young man from India (Gandhi was only 23 at this time), went up to Gandhi, and asked the young man if he could help.[70]

Mohandas Gandhi explained his anxiety. The African American said, "I have an American friend, Mr. Johnston, who has a hotel in Pretoria. He might put you up." So they walked from the station to the hotel, this man whose name is not known and Gandhi. Gandhi describes the incident in his autobiography, written 33 years later, but does not give the name of the good Samaritan. At the hotel, the man introduced Gandhi to Mr. Johnston, who said: "You can stay in the hotel if you are willing to eat in your room. If I took you to the dining room, the other guests might not like it." Gandhi hated conditions of this sort but he made the compromise. "All right," he said. A little later there was a knock on the door, and Gandhi thought it was a man with a tray. But it was Mr. Johnston himself, who said: "I have spoken to the other guests in the hotel and they are willing for you to eat in the dining room." As far as I know it was Gandhi's first encounter with Americans, one Black and the other White.[71]

Rajmohan Gandhi points out that it remains an interesting fact of history that the man who enabled Gandhi to have a roof and a bed in Pretoria was an African American.[72] As is evident from a sketch of Mohandas Gandhi's early life, he was "born to rebel." His philosophy would inevitably be a philosophy for faith in action. It was to be more than a philosophy for social engagement; it was to become a philosophy for social transformation. He came to believe that every person was of equal value, and that oppressed people should struggle for their equality. According to Gandhi, they must fight peacefully and they must not hurt others while doing so. He strongly believed that unjust laws should not be obeyed, but that people should not be violent in their attempt to change laws.

In 1907, Gandhi, who was still in South Africa, read Henry David Thoreau. In seeking to conceptualize his philosophy, Gandhi borrowed the anglicized term "civil disobedience" from Thoreau, which was more often referred to as "passive resistance." But Gandhi was not satisfied with either. Both, in his estimation, were too narrowly conceived; they appeared to be negative, passive and weak. They could easily denigrate into hatred and would likely opt, finally, for violence. Thus, civil disobedience and passive resistance became obsolete for Gandhi.

In a magazine called *Indian Opinion,* which he edited for a time in South Africa, Gandhi offered a small prize to be "awarded to the reader who invented the best designation for our struggle." One of his cousins, Maganlal Gandhi, produced a word that seemed almost right, *sadagraha,* which means "firmness in a good cause." Gandhi corrected it to *satyagraha...* *Satya* means "Truth"; *graha* means "firmness, tenacity, holding on." [73]

"I thus began," Gandhi says, "to call the Indian movement s*atyagraha,* that is to say the Force that is born in truth and love, or non-violence," and gave up the use of the phrase "passive resistance." On other occasions, Gandhi called it "Soul Force", "Love Force", or "Truth force." *Sat* in *satyagraha* means "being," "that which is," "truth." For Gandhi, *Sat* was "the only correct and fully significant name for God. [74]

The conception of s*atyagraha* became fundamental to Gandhi's life and activity. [75] It is "truth-taking" or "the taking of vows of truthfulness." Its root and meaning is "holding on to truth" and, by extension, resistance to evil by nonviolent means. This "truth force" is possible because it excludes the use of violence, because humans are capable of grasping the truth (but not in an absolute sense) and are not competent to punish. Theologically, truth in an absolute sense is God or Ultimate Being.

In Gandhi's writings, teachings and actions in South Africa, *satyagraha* became manifest as a technique for action. It is not dogma; it is neither static nor substantial. It is, rather, a dynamic and spiritual concept and a technique and process for action leading to personal and social transformation. As Gandhi saw it, s*atyagraha* is not intended to overwhelm one's opponent. It should not be used in an arbitrary way to rectify a situation. *Satyagraha* must be a last resort in an unbearable situation that merits the commitment of unlimited suffering. All would-be participants must be thoroughly prepared to know the factuality of the grievances being set forth. Participants must be willing to join in the conclusion that the cause is just and attainable, and they must be on the side of truth, which transcends facts. In other words, the truth being sought must be of such dimension that the practice of "soul-force" might give opponents concern. Opponents should be moved to seek the opportunity to change sides, and to approximate the higher goal or good that beckons all to become involved for human betterment and fulfillment.

A related concept used by Gandhi in the discussion of the meaning of nonviolent action was the principle *ahimsa* (non-injury). This term is borrowed from the Jains. Jainism, founded by Mahavira, is one of the oldest personally founded religions in India. The Jains were known for their doctrine of the non-injury of all forms of life. It was this religious concept of *ahimsa* that attracted Gandhi. Historically, Jains became merchants rather than farmers because they did not wish to destroy any form of (sentient) life. Even today, Jaina women wear veils over their noses and mouths to avoid breathing in any form of insect life.[76]

For Gandhi, *ahimsa* was the basic law of being. It can be used as the most effective principle for social action, since it is deeply ingrained in human nature and corresponds to humanity's innate desire for peace, justice, freedom and personal dignity. *Himsa* (violence or injury) is just the opposite – it degrades, corrupts and destroys. It feeds on the tendency to meet force with force, hatred with hatred. This approach leads to progressive denigration. Nonviolence, on the other hand, heals and restores humanity's best nature, while providing the best means of restoring a social order of justice and freedom. *Ahimsa* is not preoccupied with the seizure of power as an end in itself; it is a way of transforming relationships in order to bring about a peaceful transfer of power.[77]

Gandhi was convinced of the power of nonviolence, through the principles of *satyagraha* and *ahimsa,* as the key to achieving the aims of peace. In 1926, he wrote:

Nonviolence is the greatest force humanity has been endowed with. Truth is the only goal we have. For God is none other than Truth. But Truth cannot be, never will be reached except through nonviolence. That which distinguishes us from other animals is our capacity to be nonviolent. And we fulfill our mission only to the extent that we are nonviolent and no more. We have no doubt many gifts. But if we do not serve the main purpose – the development of the spirit of nonviolence in us – they but drag us down lower than the brute, a status from which we have only just emerged. The cry for peace will be a cry in the wilderness, so long as the spirit of nonviolence does not dominate millions of men and women. An armed conflict between nations horrifies us. But the economic war is no better than an armed conflict. This is like a surgical operation. An economic war is prolonged torture. And its ravages are no less terrible than those depicted in the literature on war properly so called. We think nothing of the other because we are used to its deadly effects.[78]

Gandhi's conception of nonviolence began with the spiritual disciplines of prayer, solitude and fasting. By avoiding power in all its forms of violence and control, and by renouncing the desire for immediate results, Gandhi discovered that one could be reduced to zero. From this ground zero of emptiness, the compassionate love of God - nonviolence – could grow. At this point, Gandhi intimated, the individual becomes "irresistible" and one's nonviolence becomes "all-pervasive." [79] *Satyagraha*, the power of the powerless, Gandhi believed, is the power of God, the power of truth and love that goes beyond the physical world into the realm of the spiritual. This power can overcome death, as God revealed through the nonviolence of Jesus, his crucifixion, and subsequent resurrection in the resisting community.[80]

Gandhi's experiments in Truth revealed that the mandate of the Sermon on the Mount – to love one's enemies – is of critical importance. In all of his public uses of nonviolence, he always manifested a desire for reconciliation, friendship with his opponent. He also always tried to stand with the outcasts of society and to speak up for the rights of the marginalized. In India, such solidarity primarily meant taking the radical and scandalizing public stand on behalf of the so-called untouchables, those deemed in the Indian caste system to be Dalits. Instead, Gandhi called them *harijans,* or "children of God," and begged his fellow Indians to banish untouchability from their hearts and lives.[81]

Gandhi warned against what he called the seven social sins, which ultimately served to divide society into the powerful and the powerless. He identified these social sins as: (1) politics without principle, (2) wealth without work, (3) commerce without morality, (4) pleasure without conscience, (5) education without character, (6) science without humanity, and (7) worship without sacrifice.[82] Jim Wallis, in *The Soul of Politics,* suggests that these social sins today… are the accepted practices of the life of the nation.[83]

William Shannon, in *Seeds of Peace,* asserts that no one has found an English equivalent for *satyagraha.* Hence, we are still obliged to content ourselves with the word "nonviolence." But we need continually to make clear the positive meaning it intends to convey as a translation of *ahimsa.*[84]

In summary, Mohandas Gandhi's conceptions of *satyagraha* and *ahimsa* can be capsulated in the following nine observations.

1. Mohandas Gandhi was convinced of the power of nonviolence as the key to achieving the aims of peace. In 1926, he wrote, "Nonviolence is the greatest force with which humanity has been endowed. Truth is the only goal we have. For God is none other than Truth. But Truth cannot be, never will be reached except through nonviolence."

2. In 1907, Gandhi devised the Sanskrit term *satyagraha,* with *satya* meaning "Truth", and *graha* meaning "firmness, tenacity, holding on." For Gandhi, this is Force that is born in truth and love, or non-violence." He thus gave up the use of the phrase "passive resistance." On various occasions, Gandhi called *satyagraha,* "Soul Force", "Love Force" or "Truth force."

3. The conception of *satyagraha* became fundamental to Gandhi's life and activity. It is "truth-taking" or "the taking of vows of truthfulness." Its root and meaning is "holding on to truth" and, by extension, resistance to evil by nonviolent means.

4. This "truth force" is possible because it excludes the use of violence, because humans are capable of grasping the truth (but not in an absolute sense) and are not competent to punish. Theologically, "Truth" in an absolute sense is God or Ultimate Being.

5. A related concept used by Gandhi in the discussion of the meaning of nonviolent action was the principle of *ahimsa* (non-injury). This term is borrowed from the Jains. Jainism, founded by Mahavira, is one of the oldest personally founded religions in India.

6. For Gandhi, *ahimsa* was the basic law of being. It can be used as the most effective principle for social action, since it is ingrained deeply in human nature and corresponds to humanity's innate desire for peace, justice, freedom and personal dignity. *Himsa* (violence or injury) is just the opposite – it degrades, corrupts and destroys.

7. For Gandhi, *satyagraha* was a primary technique for social action. It is not intended to overwhelm one's opponent. It should not be used in an arbitrary way to rectify a situation. *Satyagraha* must be a last resort in an unbearable situation that merits the commitment of unlimited suffering.

8. *Satyagraha and ahimsa* were critical tools for Gandhi in the fight against what he called the seven social sins, which served ultimately to divide society into the powerful and the powerless. He identified these social sins as: (1) politics without principle, (2) wealth without

work, (3) commerce without morality, (4) pleasure without conscience, (5) education without character, (6) science without humanity, and (7) worship without sacrifice.

9. Gandhi's concept of *satyagraha,* or Truth-Force, was understood almost immediately as "love-force" by Martin Luther King, Jr. and others. Howard Thurman, like King and others saw a direct connection between Truth and Love, and like Gandhi, essentially equated the two. They saw in Gandhi the means by which the love-ethic in the teachings of Jesus – especially in the Sermon on the Mount - could become effective for social transformation. King stated, "As I read, I became fascinated by (Gandhi's) campaigns of nonviolent resistance.... The whole concept of *satyagraha...*was profoundly significant to me... I came to feel that this was the only morally and practically sound method open to oppressed people in their struggle for freedom."

   In Mohandas Gandhi's writings, teachings and actions, *satyagraha* and *ahimsa* became manifest as principled tools for action toward nonviolence, peacemaking, community-building and a love-ethic that could lead toward spiritual and social transformation. These constructs are not dogmatic, and neither are they static. Rather, they are dynamic and spiritual concepts, techniques and processes for action. Amidst violence, wars, terror and various other forms of social disintegration that afflict society today, *satyagraha* and *ahimsa* can serve as means of helping humanity move towards higher goals of the common good, nonviolence, peace with justice, and inclusive community that beckon all persons to become involved in the quest for human betterment and fulfillment.

C. *The Application of Satyagraha, Ahimsa and Nonviolence*

Gandhi saw national self-respect as a religious and spiritual virtue. India was the embodiment of such truth and virtue to him. However, he knew well that national self-respect could cloak cruelty and hatred. He was a strong Indian nationalist. He said in 1940: "my mission is to convert every Indian, whether he is a Hindu, Muslim or any other, even Englishmen and finally the world to nonviolence for regulating mutual relations whether political, economic, social or religious." The phrase "even ...and finally" revealed his priority towards serving and leading Indians to liberation. "I can't find Him apart from the rest of humanity," he said. "My countrymen," he added, "are my nearest neighbors." He had to serve people if he was to serve God; and his nearest neighbors were Indians. He said in 1931, "My nationalism, fierce though it is, is not exclusive, is not devised to harm any nation or individual." A core of nationalism always resided in him, rallying Indians, inspiring colonized people everywhere to rise above the social ill and violence that was so much a part of Indian reality under British domination.[85]

Gandhi realized that the spirituality of nonviolence begins within persons, and moves out from there. The life of active nonviolence is the fruit of an inner peace and spiritual unity already realized in us, and not the other way around... through our personal, inner conversion, our own inner peace, we are sensitized to care for God, ourselves, each other, for the poor, and for the world. Gandhi taught that nonviolence does not mean passivity. It is the most daring, creative and courageous way of living, and it is the only hope for the world. Nonviolence demands creativity. It pursues dialogue, seeks reconciliation, listens to the truth in opponents, rejects militarism, and allows God's Spirit to transform us socially and politically.[86]

Nonviolence is the essence of truth; one cannot seek truth, Gandhi discovered, and continue to participate in violence and injustice within one's heart and in the world. Nonviolence is the power of the powerless, the power of God, the only power that overcomes evil. "Nonviolence is the greatest and most active force in the world... One person who can express nonviolence in life exercises a force superior to all the forces of brutality... It cannot be preached. It has to be practiced," Gandhi insisted. "If we remain nonviolent, hatred will die as everything does, from disuse."[87]

The first commitment of a nonviolent person is to the truth, according to Gandhi. Quoted by Thomas Merton, Gandhi sums up the heart of his teaching about nonviolence: "The way of peace is the way of truth." He even says: "Truthfulness is more important than peacefulness... A truthful person cannot long remain violent." Gandhi offered his reason for saying this: "A person will perceive in the course of his research that he has no need to be violent, and he will further discover that so long as there is the slightest trace of violence in him, he will fail to find the truth he is searching for." At the deepest level of our being we are in touch with God and therefore with truth itself. That is why at the core of our being we are nonviolent..." [88]

Gandhi viewed the problem of violence as being rooted in the hearts of men and women. Thus, the means of realizing nonviolence and peace were through transforming the hearts of persons. In 1926, he stated:

I observe, in the limited field in which I find myself, that unless I can reach the hearts of men and women, I am able to do nothing. I observe further that so long as the spirit of hate persists in some shape or other, it is impossible to establish peace or to gain our freedom by peaceful effort. We cannot love one another if we hate Englishmen. We cannot love the Japanese and hate the Englishmen. We must either let the law of love rule us through and through or not at all. Love among ourselves based on hatred of others breaks down under the slightest pressure. The fact is, such love is never real love. It is an armed peace. And so it will be in this great movement in the West against war. War will only be stopped when the conscience of humankind has become sufficiently elevated to recognize the undisputed supremacy of the Law of Love in all the walks of life. Some say this will never come to pass. I shall retain the faith till the end of my earthly existence that it shall come to pass.[89]

In 1929, Dr. John Mott met Gandhi in India. Mott asked: "What causes you solicitude, concern, for the future of India?" That was on the eve of Gandhi's Salt March to the Sea, so that Gandhi was close to a high point on his freedom movement. He responded: "Our apathy and hardness of heart, if I may use the biblical phrase, toward the masses and their poverty."[90]

Mott also asked him about what India was meant to contribute to the world. Gandhi answered: "Nonviolence, which the country is exhibiting at the present day on a scale unprecedented in history." He added that nonviolence has "so permeated our people that an armed revolution has almost become an impossibility in India, not because, as some would have it, we as a race are physically weak, for it does not require much physical strength so much as a devilish will to press a trigger to shoot a person, but because the traditions of *ahimsa* (nonviolence/non-injury) have struck deep roots among the people."

In 1945, Deton Brooks of the *Chicago Defender* was one of two African Americans to meet with Gandhi. Brooks asked Gandhi if he had a message for America. In his well-known answer, Gandhi said, "My life is its message." Also in the summer of 1945, a man named Frank E. Bolden of the National Negro Press Association went to interview Gandhi, who however, interviewed Bolden on the condition of Blacks in the United States. Wrote Bolden on Gandhi's reaction to the story: "All during our discussion I noticed the great Mahatma's face registering first sorrow, then disgust, then agreement, followed by humor, and ending in pleasure."[91]

Once, two of Gandhi's close friends, Charles F. Andrews and Rabindranath Tagore, who had won a Nobel Prize for literature in 1913, expressed their unhappiness at one of Gandhi's methods in the nonviolent battle for freedom: the burning of foreign cloth. Tagore and Andrews said to Gandhi: "How can you do this? You are burning something valuable and beautiful." Gandhi gave his answer: "I want to care for the starving Indian peasant. He has nothing. I want him to spin and weave and to make cloth. Nobody will buy his cloth if mass-produced cloth from Manchester is sold in India." Also, said Gandhi: "Indians hate the British. I want to deflect their hate from people to things."

It is known that some Christians in England strongly urged Gandhi to convert to Christianity. He did read the Bible carefully. He found the Old Testament to be more difficult than the New Testament. Jesus, and the Sermon on the Mount, impressed Gandhi more than any other part of the Christian Scriptures. However, he never was convinced that it was necessary to abandon Hinduism for Christianity. He could not accept Christianity as a perfect religion. Gandhi also saw defects in Hinduism but, for him, Hinduism was all that was necessary to satisfy his soul. He had some leanings toward Christianity, but was never moved to make an all-out commitment to it.

Nevertheless, throughout his life, Gandhi was able to defend the best that he had gleaned from the study of Christianity. He urged people to live more like Jesus Christ, practice the Christian faith without adulterating it or toning it down, and to emphasize love and make it the driving force of life and action. It is not surprising that Gandhi asserted that his encounter with Christianity made him a better Hindu. His attention to some of the noblest principles of Christianity enriched his life as a religious person. Although he remained a Hindu, his understanding and expression of religious experience was more profound due to his engagement with Christianity.

II. Gandhi's Influence on Howard Thurman

Howard Thurman was among the leading American Christian religious figures attracted to the thinking and praxis of Mohandas Gandhi. Thurman was extremely impressed with Gandhi's ideas on the power of nonviolence as a method which positively responds to the spiritual needs of humanity, while at the same time accomplishing the necessary political transformation of the social order.[92] Certainly, Gandhi's success in India was solid evidence for nonviolence. Thurman's engagement with Gandhi would serve to reinforce, confirm and provide deeper insights about the efficacy of

50

nonviolence in the search for common ground and radically inclusive community in the American churches and society.

In 1935, during his tenure at Howard University, Thurman, then the Dean at Rankin Chapel at Howard University, and his wife Sue Bailey Thurman were asked to be members of a delegation on a "Pilgrimage of Friendship" to India, Ceylon and Burma. Thurman's participation was considered important because "in a country divided by religious beliefs into 'Touchables' and 'Untouchables', rich and poor, the testimony of representatives from another country's minority group might be far-reaching."[93]

Thurman and the delegation lectured and discussed issues at 45 academic centers in these three countries from October 1935 through the spring of 1936. He was questioned continually about the compatibility of Christianity with black people's struggle for human dignity. White Christians and churches had a history of being insensitive to black people's worth and freedom. Thurman answered these queries by distinguishing Christianity from the religion of Jesus. Despite this clarification, he admits that:

> All answers had to be defensive because there was not a single instance known to me in which a local church had a completely integrated membership. The color bar was honored in the practice of the Christian religion. From a 10,000-mile perspective, this monumental betrayal of the Christian ethic loomed large and forbidding.[94]

It was out of this background that Thurman had a religious experience at the Khyber Pass (between Afghanistan and West Pakistan) which excited a vision that would determine the thrust of his spiritual and social witness for the rest of his life. Thurman wrote:

51

We saw clearly what we must do somehow when we returned to America. We knew that we must test whether a religious fellowship could be developed in America that was capable of cutting across all racial barriers, with a carryover into the common life, a fellowship that would alter the behavior patterns of those involved. It became imperative now to find out if experiences of spiritual unity among people could be more compelling than the experiences which divide them.[95]

While on this trip, Howard and his wife Sue Bailey Thurman, along with Rev. and Mrs. Edward and Phenola Carroll had asked for a chance to visit with Gandhi. (Rev. Edward Carroll would eventually become one of the first African-American bishops in the United Methodist Church). Gandhi had written welcoming them. Remarkably, Gandhi broke his fast for the duration of the delegation's visit. The delegation met for several hours with Gandhi in Bardoli, India. When the four Americans arrived, Gandhi went out of his way to greet them. He didn't always do that to visitors. His secretary, Mahadev Desai, told Thurman that he had never seen Gandhi greet a visitor so warmly in his many years with Gandhi.

By all accounts, Thurman's conversation with Gandhi represented the first formal exchange between an African-American religious leader and the great Indian prophet of nonviolent revolution. It was Gandhi's first opportunity to engage African Americans in discussion concerning their respective struggles for freedom. An outspoken critic of traditional Christianity, Gandhi believed that western interpretations of Christianity contributed to racial, economic and gender discrimination, and led to segregation of the world's people.

The encounter became a profound aspect of Gandhi's spiritual life, offering him a view of Christianity which was, in many ways, transformational. In the course of their discussion, which was largely centered on Gandhi's questions posed to Thurman concerning Christianity, parallels between the caste system of Hinduism and the exclusivity in the praxis of Christianity became apparent.

On the visit, Thurman asked Gandhi to define nonviolence. Gandhi said he hoped it would be love in the Pauline sense, love as spelled out in the letter to the Corinthians, plus the struggle for justice. Thurman also asked Gandhi whether South African blacks had joined his nonviolence movement. Gandhi replied: "No, they hadn't." He said he deliberately did not want to amalgamate those two struggles at that time. He added that this was due to their lack of understanding of the meaning and methods of nonviolence. But Gandhi's work there had an impact on influential leaders in South Africa such as Albert Luthuli who, like Martin Luther King, Jr. was awarded the Nobel Peace Prize.

Thurman later recalled that Gandhi asked persistent, pragmatic questions about American Negroes, about the course of slavery, and how they had survived it.[96] Gandhi asked about the plight of blacks in the United States with respect to issues such as economics, interracial marriage and politics.

In the course of his discussion with Gandhi, Thurman recalled the following, "One of the things that puzzled him (Gandhi) was why the slaves did not become Moslems. "Because", said Gandhi, "the Moslem religion is the only religion in the world in which no lines are drawn from within the religious fellowship. Once you are in, you are all the way in. This is not true in Christianity, it isn't true in Buddhism or Hinduism. If you had become Moslem, then even though you were a slave, in the faith you would be equal to your master."[97]

Gandhi asked his American visitors if they would sing a Negro spiritual for him. Gandhi was greatly moved as Mrs. Sue Bailey Thurman sang two familiar Negro spirituals: "Were You There When They Crucified My Lord" and "We Are Climbing Jacob's Ladder." To all who heard them, these spirituals expressed the hopes and aspirations of the oppressed to climb higher and higher until freedom's goal has been reached.[98]

After hearing these spirituals, Gandhi said to the four: "Well if it comes true, it may be through the Negroes (in America) that the unadulterated message of nonviolence will be delivered to the world."[99] In other words, by this time in 1936, Gandhi was not sure that it would be India that would deliver a model of nonviolence to the world, and he gave expression to a prophetic intuition that African Americans would demonstrate nonviolence on a global scale.

The conversation between Thurman and Gandhi continued. Thurman inquired further about the nature of nonviolence. Gandhi replied:

> … without direct, active expression of it, nonviolence to my mind is meaningless. One cannot be passively nonviolent. In fact, nonviolence is a term I had to coin in order to bring out the root meaning of *ahimsa*. In spite of the negative particle "non," it is no negative force. Superficially, we are surrounded in life by strife and bloodshed, life living upon life. But some great seer, who ages ago penetrated the center of truth, said, "It is not through strife and violence but through nonviolence that man fulfills his destiny and his duty to his fellow creatures." It is a force that is more positive

than electricity, and more powerful than either. At the center of nonviolence is the force, which is self-acting. *Ahisma* means "love" in the Pauline sense, and yet something more than love defined by St. Paul, although I know St. Paul's beautiful definition is good enough for all practical purposes. *Ahisma* includes the whole creation, and not only humans.[100]

Thurman asked: "How are we to train individuals and communities in this difficult act?" Gandhi replied:

… through great study, tremendous perseverance, and thorough cleansing of one's self of all impurities. If for mastering the physical sciences you have to devote a whole lifetime, how many lifetimes may be needed for mastering the greatest spiritual force that mankind has ever known? But why worry even if it means several lifetimes? For, if this is the only permanent thing in life, if it is the only thing that counts, then whatever effort you bestow on mastering it is well spent. "Seek ye first the Kingdom of Heaven and everything else will be added unto you." The Kingdom of Heaven is *ahimsa.*[101]

Sue Bailey Thurman asked, "How am I to act, supposing my own brother was being lynched before my very eyes?" Gandhi responded:

There is such a thing as self-immolation. Supposing I was a Negro, and my sister was ravished by a white and lynched by a whole community, what would be my duty? I ask myself. And the answer comes to me: I must not wish ill to these, but neither must I cooperate with them. It may be that ordinarily I depend on the lynching community for my livelihood. I refuse to cooperate with them, refuse to touch food that comes from them, and I refuse to cooperate with even my brother Negroes who tolerate the wrong. This is the self-immolation that I mean. I have often in my life resorted to this plan. Of course, a mechanical act of starvation will mean nothing. One's faith must remain undimmed while one's life ebbs out minute by minute.[102]

In formulating his response to Gandhi's critique of Christianity, Thurman began to integrate Gandhian principles of unity and nonviolent social change into his own Christian pacifism and mysticism.[103] Thurman returned to the United States with "an enhanced interpretation of the meaning of nonviolence."[104] From Gandhi, "a man who (was) rooted in the basic mysticism of the [Hindu] Brahma," Thurman learned the life-affirming concepts of *ahimsa* and *satyagraha*. He found in Gandhi a kindred mind and spirit who refused to think in terms of a disconnected Truth, God, or Ultimate reality but focused his attention on that which was pre-eminently practical and spiritual.[105]

The end result of the conversation was that Thurman felt assured that nonviolence, as expressed in Gandhian principles and practice, could transform whatever difficulties it confronted. The techniques might have to be refined, individuals would need to go through radical preparation to be faithful disciples of the method, large numbers of people might suffer and die, but the moral and spiritual imperatives for nonviolence would prevail over experiences of violence.[106]

In a sense, the trip to South Asia provided a crucial global context and served as a catalyst for Thurman's understanding of the relationships among what was for him authentic religion, inclusive community and human suffering. Here, he was confronted with the tension of political and social patterns of exclusion that rivaled racial discrimination in America. He discovered that the Hindu Untouchable and the African-American alike were bound in their subordinate status. Equally unsettling was the fact that religion and culture had conjoined to legitimate and encourage this sordid quarantine. [107]

Indeed, an important contribution that Gandhi made to Thurman's work was in offering a global perspective on the human condition. The anti-imperialist movement then surging through South Asia, exemplified by the implementation of ethical nonviolence and non-cooperation on the part of the masses, provided the first critical international referent for Thurman's understanding of the relationship that exists between religion and the social world. Thurman's wartime essay, "The Fascist Masquerade," offers a glimpse into this aspect of his development.[108] Later, other arenas of protest – colonial Africa, Nazi Germany, the Native American communities of Canada and the United States – would further sensitize Thurman's thinking in this regard.

Upon leaving India, especially motivated by a deep spiritual experience at the Khyber Pass, Thurman realized that an influx of new ideas and new ways of seeing was necessary if Christianity and the religion of Jesus were to approach oneness and radical forms of inclusive community.

Thurman returned to Howard University convinced that a religious fellowship in America had to be conceived which would unite persons across social and creedal divisions. At Howard, he began to experiment with the arts, meditation, and innovative liturgies to create worship experiences which affirmed the unity within the audiences, and which had religious, social and philosophical diversity. These creative experiences were designed to evoke religious feelings that magnified the essence of religion, as opposed to reinforcing religious dogmas and creeds that emphasized divisive differences. Audience members were not to be perceived as objects for theological discourse, but as subjects of religious experience. A common religious experience had the potential to transcend and diminish the meaning of all that separates.[109]

For Gandhi and Thurman, community is not built on presupposed division, but on the basic unity of humankind. It is not out for the conversion of the wicked to the ideas of the good, but for healing reconciliation.[110] As Gandhi saw it, the full consistent practice of nonviolence and peace demands a solid metaphysical and religious basis both in being and in God. This comes before subjective good intentions and sincerity. For the Hindu, this metaphysical basis was provided by the Vedantist doctrine of the Atman, the true transcendent Self which alone is absolutely real, and before which the empirical self of the individual must be effaced in the faithful practice of dharma.[111]

In the final analysis, for Mohandas Gandhi, *satyagraha* and *ahimsa* became the principles and necessary techniques for movement toward nonviolence, community-building and social transformation. Amidst division and segregation that remain extant in the world today, *satyagraha* and *ahimsa* can serve as means of helping humanity move toward goals of the common ground, common good and radically inclusive community.

CHAPTER THREE
HOWARD THURMAN AND THE IDENTITY OF JESUS

"The Christian Church has tended to overlook its Judaic origins, but the fact is that Jesus of Nazareth was a Jew of Palestine when he went about his Father's business, announcing the acceptable year of the Lord."
- Howard Thurman

Howard Thurman's Christology was rooted in his experiences of being personally victimized by racism and oppression. He was acutely aware that racism and other forms of social disintegration attacked his self-worth and freedom. His mystical experiences, however, provided the assurance that he was a beloved child of God, and that harmonious relatedness is the underlying structure of reality. He was aware that racism denied the truth about God's intent for creation. It put the welfare of the community in crisis. The prophetic questions for him became: How could he help shape a social reality that conformed to his religious beliefs? How could he speak to the crisis of humanity by restoring the community's (especially America's) sense of well-being.[112]

In Thurman's mind, Jesus of Nazareth is the revelation of how personality creates community; Jesus personifies the transforming power of love. The conditions and circumstances of Jesus' life are significant in understanding Christianity and the meaning of Jesus in the world.[113]

Thurman began to fully outline the basic principles of his Christology in the early part of 1935 at the annual convocation on preaching at the School of Theology of Boston University.[114] Subsequently in 1948, he delivered a series of lectures at Huston College (now Huston-Tillotson College) in Austin, Texas, and in 1949 published, *Jesus and the Disinherited,* which gave a radical perspective of the mission, ministry and teachings of Jesus, as compared with the general view of the majority of the theologians and churches of that time. Here, Thurman essentially exegetes the life and person of Jesus of Nazareth. Throughout, Thurman showed that Jesus' ministry in the world focused on addressing the needs and aspirations of the disinherited. He argued that the concern of Jesus is still for the disinherited.[115]

Early in this seminal work, Thurman intimated that "many and varied are the interpretations dealing with the teachings and life of Jesus of Nazareth, but few of these interpretations deal with what the teachings and life of Jesus have to say to those who stand, at a moment in human history with their backs against the wall."[116]

Thurman further asserted that it was among the disinherited that Jesus chose to realize the message of the Gospel, not at the centers of power but among the disenfranchised and powerless. He presented a Jesus who counted himself as part of an oppressed minority, realizing that true freedom was not obtained by somehow conquering or altering external circumstances but through inward transformation. In the midst of suffering, it was possible to experience the liberation which no outside force can penetrate. Thurman reflected upon the message of Jesus given to those he came to liberate in this way: "His message focused on the urgency of a radical change in the inner attitude of the people. Jesus fully recognized that out of the heart are the issues of life and that no external force, however great and overwhelming, can at long last destroy a people if it does not first win the victory of the spirit against them."[117]

Thurman also emphasized the social circumstances of this poor and oppressed Palestinian Jew, and then concluded that the religion of Jesus was a creative response which emerged from and dealt with transforming these conditions of oppression and sought to develop radically inclusive community. Thurman set forth to paint a picture, an image of Jesus, that reveals God in Christ in a way that God is always on the side of the oppressed, and also is always working and acting on behalf of the oppressed. Jesus most clearly expressed this concern in Luke 4:18-19, where he said, "The Spirit of the Lord is on me, because he has anointed me to proclaim good news to the poor. He has sent me to proclaim freedom for the prisoners and recovery of sight for the blind, to set the oppressed free..."

Thurman devoted a major portion of *Jesus and the Disinherited* to addressing the nature of Christian witness. He indicated how Jesus used the Parable of the Good Samaritan to reveal how the love of neighbor should respond directly to human need, permitting no barriers of class, race, and condition.[118]

He asserted that, "Every man is potentially every other man's neighbor."[119] Jesus practiced love not only for those who acted as personal enemies, but also for persons who made it difficult for the Israelites to live without shame and humiliation. In Jesus' day, tax collectors helped perpetuate the Roman oppression of Israel. They were despised for helping the enemy, and to be seen in their company meant the loss of status and respect in the community.[120] Yet Jesus invited Matthew, a tax collector to become his disciple. Thurman wrote:

> When Jesus became a friend to the tax collectors and secured one as his companion, it was a spiritual triumph

of such staggering proportions that after nineteen hundred years it defies rational explanation.[121]

Thurman maintained that in every ghetto and dwelling place of the disinherited throughout the ages, there have been those who have tried to prosper by the betrayal of their own people:

> To love such people requires the uprooting of the bitterness of betrayal, the heartiest poison that grows in the human spirit... To love them means to recognize some deep respect and reverence for their persons. But to love them does not mean to condone their way of life.[122]

He emphasized that the love that Jesus practiced extended also to the Roman, the political enemy of Israel. When Jesus spoke with the Roman captain who sought healing for his servant, Jesus claimed that he had not found such faith in all of Israel. Thurman explained that in this encounter, the Roman, in seeking help from a Jewish teacher, put aside his status as a Roman, and Jesus did not regard him as an enemy but as a human being:

> The concept of reverence for personality then is applicable between persons from whom, in their initial instance, the heavy weight of status has been sloughed off. Then what? Each person meets the other where he is and there treats him as if he were where he ought to be. Here we emerge into an area where love operates, revealing a universal characteristic unbounded by special or limited circumstances.[123]

Thurman sought to explicate the ethical insights of the Jewish prophets, as interpreted through the life of Jesus. He pointed out that the ethical example of Jesus continues to have relevance for people who find themselves backed up against the wall. How ought the impoverished ethnic and religious minorities respond to the material and spiritual assaults of imperial oppression? The example of Jesus suggests a response of courage, truth telling, and love. [124]

For Thurman, there was no possibility of community without careful and constructive attention to the *disinherited* of whom Jesus was concerned. He proclaimed that the mistreatment of America's *disinherited* and acceptance of "the will to segregate" are betrayals of American and Christian ideals of community-building. He explored the plight of the disinherited as it relates to those denied a rightful place in human society. He reflected by intimating with the following, "the awareness of being a child of God tends to stabilize the ego and results in a new courage, fearlessness, and power..." "such a man realizes that death cannot possibly be the worst thing in the world. There are some things that are worse than death. To deny one's own integrity of personality in the presence of human challenge is one of those things."[125]

Thurman concluded that love is the force that affirms full humanity and creates full, radically inclusive community, and that nonviolent change is the best expression of love. He considered the terms "reconciliation" and "love" to be synonymous.[126] He defined love as "the intelligent, kindly but stern expression of kinship of one individual for another, having as its purpose the maintenance and furtherance of life at its highest level."[127] Love responds to an individual's basic need of being cared for. It participates in the attempt to actualize potential, and therefore completes the fragmented and unfulfilled personality. But on a larger scale, it brings together separated lives. It makes apparent the significance of relationships by stressing how inter-dependence is inherent in all of life. Love creates community.[128]

Howard Thurman and the Humanity of Christ

Howard Thurman's Christology depicts Jesus who is flesh and blood – God incarnate - who lived in a contextual reality like many oppressed people live, and yet who emerged from it whole, and calls us to that same reality and empowers us for daily living. Indeed, Thurman's is a contextualized Christology, especially as it regards the oppressed and disinherited. His Christology is of a present, powerful and personal Christ who not only saves us from sin into eternal life, but redeems us to be change agents in the world, modeling Jesus before others. It is to this that we are called, and it is for this that we are empowered.

Jesus of Nazareth was among the very poor; his mother was an unwed teenager, and his earthly father was a homeless carpenter. As it regards Jesus' social location, Thurman, in *The Mood of Christmas* posited:

But the important thing is that to the mother of Jesus he was a baby boy who grew hungry, who had to be fed, bathed, nurtured, and who had to be given tender loving care, one who pulled at her heartstrings and who became so much a part of her sense of worth and meaning, that she was sure, in a sense, that this was the first baby in the world... We must do our part to guarantee that all children may have the chance to be children, to experience their own childhood. If this does not happen to them, they will be forced to deal with their environment as if they were adults.[129]

Thurman focused on the humanity of Jesus from his birth. Thurman further asserted:

> Stripped bare of art forms and liturgy, the literal substance of the story remains, Jesus Christ was born in a stable, he was born of humble parentage in surroundings that are the common lot of those who earn their living by the sweat of their brows. Nothing can rob the common (person) of this heritage - when we behold Jesus, we see in him the possibilities of life even for the humblest and a dramatic resolution of the meaning of God.[130]

Thurman went on to state:

> In Jesus, all (persons) may see the illumined finger of God guiding them in the way that they should go, so that high above the clash of arms in the conflict for status, for place, for privilege, for rights, (we) can hear speaking distinctly and clearly to our own spirit the still small voice of God, without which nothing has real meaning, with which all the rest of the journey, however difficult, however painful, however devastating, will be filled with a music all its own and even the stars in their appointed rounds and all the wooded world of nature participate in the triumphant music of our hearts."[131]

Thurman and the Crucifixion of Christ

It is the cross and resurrection of Christ that gives ultimate expression to concerns of human liberation. The cross

(Christ's crucifixion) provides a unique angle of vision for understanding the multidimensionality and universality of human suffering. The resurrection symbolizes the promise of new possibilities for meaning, life and hope in the midst of and beyond the existential sense of dread and despair. This serves as an alternative to meaninglessness, lovelessness, hopelessness and nihilism.

In Christ, there is evidence of God's breaking into history to transform suffering into wholeness - to move persons from victims to liberated change agents. In Christ, God has spoken against evil and injustice. In Christ, the oppressed are set free to struggle against injustice, and humanity is liberated to move beyond suffering and oppression, and towards an appropriation of hope and life. In the cross and empty tomb is evidence of the reality that "death has been swallowed up in victory" (1 Cor. 15:54), that hope overcomes despair, that peace with justice is possible amidst injustice, and that liberation and transformation may be realized amidst oppression. In the cross and resurrection is evidence that life is ultimately possible amidst impending death.

Thurman's views on the cross and resurrection are similar to those of Dietrich Bonhoeffer. In *Meditations on the Cross*, Bonhoeffer intimated that the cross wasthought to have been the end, the death of the Son of God, curse and judgment upon all flesh. If the cross were the last word on Jesus, the world would be lost in death and damnation without hope, and the world would have been victorious over God. But God, who alone effected salvation for us – "all this is from God" (2 Cor. 5:18) – raised Christ from the dead. That was the new beginning following the end as a miracle from above, though not like the springtime according to a fixed natural law, but rather according to the incomparable freedom and power of God that shatters death.[132]

Bonhoeffer pointed to Jesus' life and crucifixion as clear evidence of God's prerogative for the disinherited. God enters the world, at once to bring redemption and judgment. God enters the world to renew the world, and in renewing it God must both judge it and redeem it. In his incarnate life, Christ condemned the world and oppression through his own suffering. Jesus' life as a suffering servant of God and death on the cross is a condemnation of the norms of oppressive ways of living. Bonhoeffer reflects that Jesus "lived in deep poverty, unmarried, and died as a criminal."[133]

Thurman was one of the first Christian theologians to tie the suffering and crucifixion of Christ to the history of Black suffering in America. He asserted that aligned with the crucifixion of Christ, death was a fact, inescapable, persistent for slaves in America. For the slave, it was extremely compelling because of the cheapness with which (their) life was regarded. The slave was a tool, a thing, a utility, a commodity, but (they were) not a person. They were faced constantly with the imminent threat of death, of which the terrible overseer was the symbol; and the awareness that (the slave) was only chattel property... If a slave were killed, it was merely property loss, a matter of bookkeeping. The notion of personality, of human beings as ends so basic to the genius of the Christian faith, had no authentic application in the relationship between the slave and master. The social and religious climates were uncongenial to such an ethic.[134]

Thurman's thinking on the cross and crucifixion is resonant with the later thinking of James Cone, who in *The Cross and the Lynching Tree* intimated that "The real scandal of the gospel is this: humanity's salvation is revealed in the cross of the condemned criminal Jesus, and humanity's salvation is available only through our solidarity with the crucified people in our midst."[135] In *The Cross and the Lynching Tree,* one can see Thurman's influence on Cone's thinking about Christology. Luther Smith writes that Thurman sees that "the problem of an excluding church is rooted in the fact that too many Christians have not clearly understood or faithfully followed the central personality of the faith, Jesus the Christ."

Regarding the cross, Cone further asserted that:

> To understand what the cross means in America, we need to take a look at the lynching tree in this nation's history—that "strange (fruit) and bitter crop" that Billie Holiday would not let us forget. The lynched black victim experienced the same fate as the crucified Christ and thus became the most potent symbol for understanding the true meaning of the salvation achieved through "God on the Cross." Nietzsche was right: Christianity is a religion of slaves. God became a slave in Jesus and thereby liberated slaves from being determined by their social condition."[136]

Cone further intimated that, "Until we can see the cross and the lynching tree together, until we can identify Christ with the "re-crucified" black body hanging from a lynching tree, there can be no genuine understanding of Christian identity in America, and no deliverance from the legacy of slavery and white supremacy."[137]

In her book, *Stand Your Ground: Black Bodies and the Justice of God,* Kelly Brown Douglas offers contemporary perspective on the implications of the crucifixion and the problem of racism. She posits that disembodiment of black humanity can be seen through both the crucifixion of Jesus on the Cross, and the death of Trayvon Martin in Florida in 2012. "Both Jesus and Trayvon were members of despised minorities. Both were feared because of who they were... Both were accused of sedition. Both were killed by the "rule of law"[138].

Jesus and the Quest for Community

For Thurman, there was no possibility of community without careful and constructive attention to the disinherited. In his analysis, the mistreatment of the disinherited is rooted in hatred. He asserted that Jesus rejected hatred because he saw that hatred meant death to the mind, death to the spirit, and death to communion with his Father. Jesus affirmed life; and hatred was the great denial.

Hate is bred by fear of the "other" and comes as a by-product of the will to engage in ongoing contact without fellowship. In order for love to exist, hate must be expunged. Love and hate can't exist in the same space. Love comes on the long road where there is contact with the "other" that involves authentic fellowship.

Amidst evil and oppression - the imperative for the church to speak out and act out with prophetic clarity becomes even more critical. Throughout history, people of prophetic goodwill and conscious have seen Jesus of Nazareth as the model of speaking real truth to power, speaking truth in love, and refusing to be silenced.

In his book, *The Politics of Jesus: Rediscovering the True Revolutionary Nature of Jesus' Teachings and How They Have Been Corrupted,* Obery Hendricks argues that by the nature of who he was, and how he ministered, Jesus was a prophetic and political figure. Hendricks writes, "To say that Jesus was a political revolutionary is to say that the message he proclaimed not only called for change in individual hearts but also demanded sweeping and comprehensive change in the political, social and economic structures in his setting in life..."[139] Hendricks proposes that seven political strategies characterize the revolutionary politics of Jesus. These strategies are: 1. Treat people's needs as holy. 2. Give a voice to the voiceless. 3. Expose the working of oppression. 4. Call the demon by name. 5. Save your anger for the mistreatment of others. 6. Take blows without returning them. 7. Don't just explain the alternative, show it. [140]

Amidst racism and other forms of hated, Thurman maintained that the religion of Jesus makes the love-ethic and the quest for radically inclusive community central. Regarding this, Thurman stated that this quest is no ordinary achievement. It seems clear that Jesus started out with the simple teaching concerning love embodied in the timeless words of Israel: "Hear, O Israel: The Lord our God is one Lord: and thou shalt love the Lord thy God with all thy heart, and with all thy soul, and with all thy might," and "thy neighbor as thyself." Once the neighbor is defined, then one's moral obligation is clear.[141]

Thurman identified community as the single most important quest of human life. It had occupied his thoughts and activities since childhood. Defining and appropriating community was the end purpose (the telos) of Thurman's theology, with Christian love being the means – the instrument – for the realization of community. Establishing community was the commitment and labor of his ministry. [142] The basic principle behind Thurman's concept of community was that "the literal fact of the underlying unity of life seems to be established beyond doubt." He intimated:

> If life has been fashioned out of a fundamental unity and ground, and if it has developed within a structure, then it

is not to be wondered at that the interest in and concern for wholeness should be part of the conscious intent of life, more basic than any particular conscious tendency toward fragmentation... It (reconciliation) seeks to effect and further harmonize relations in a totally comprehensive climate.[143]

He concluded that love is the unitive force that creates community, and nonviolent change is the best expression of love. He wrote about tiny rootlets breaking through dry, cracked wastelands of hatred, tiny rootlets of kindness, love, gratitude, generosity, and fairness breaking through.

For Thurman, true community is also the clearest manifestation of salvation. The essence of Christian life is to lead individuals and communities toward wholeness *(shalom).* Christian wholeness – according to Thurman – is ultimately the movement toward "perfect community."

He understood racism as the ultimate expression of hate, and to be a contradiction to life (the teachings of Jesus).[144] Racism is inimical to the formation of identity. Neither blacks nor whites can attain a proper sense of self and give full expression to their potential in an environment of prejudice, segregation and violence. Racism is also inimical to the formation of community. Systematic discrimination sabotages the function of community as a place of nurture and growth through cooperation. Destructive forces are released to rupture life's inter-relatedness.[145]

Thurman wrote of the need to overcome hatred as a prerequisite for overcoming racism and building community.[146] His construct for understanding hatred begins in a situation where there is *contact without fellowship*. This is contact that is devoid of any of the primary overtures of warmth, fellow-feelings and genuineness. Secondly, he pointed out that contacts without fellowship tend to express themselves in the kind of *understanding that is strikingly unsympathetic.* There is understanding of a kind, but it is without healing and reinforcement of personality. Thirdly, he pointed out that unsympathetic understanding tends to express itself in the *active functioning of ill-will.*

To make this point, he shared the story of once traveling from Chicago to Memphis, Tennessee.[147] He found his seat on the train across from an elderly lady, who took immediate cognizance of his presence. When the conductor came along for the tickets, she said to him, pointing in Thurman's direction, "What is *that* doing in this car?"

The conductor answered, with a touch of creative humor, "*That* has a ticket."

For the next fifty miles, this lady talked for five or ten minutes to all who were seated in that coach, setting forth her philosophy of human relationships and the basis of her objection to Thurman's presence in the car. Thurman said that he was able to see the atmosphere of the entire car shift from common indifference to active recognition of and, to some extent positive resentment of his presence in the car. He concluded that, "An ill will spreading is like a contagious virus."

Fourth, Thurman posited that active ill-will, when dramatized in a human being, becomes *hatred walking on earth.*

He believed that the Christian love-ethic was a means by which hate such as this could be contradicted. He offered the story of the Good Samaritan as an example of how the love-ethic works:

In a memorable story Jesus defined the neighbor by telling of the Good Samaritan. With sure artistry and great power he depicted what happens when a man responds directly to human need across the barriers of class, race, and condition. Every man is potentially every other man's neighbor. Neighborliness is non-spatial, it is qualitative. A man must love his neighbor directly, clearly, permitting no barriers between.[148]

Thurman spoke of the difficulties faced by Jesus in attempting to teach and live out this love-ethic:

This was not an easy position for Jesus to take within his own community. Opposition to his teaching increased as the days passed. A twofold demand was made upon him at all times: to love those of the household of Israel who became his enemies because they regarded him as a careless perverter of the truths of God; to love those beyond the household of Israel – the Samaritan and even the Roman.[149]

Thurman's personal encounters with racism would serve to strengthen his resolve for community. He shared:

I know that the experiences of unity in human relations are more compelling than the concepts, the fears, the prejudices, which divide. Despite the tendency to feel my race superior, my nation the greatest nation, my faith the true faith, I must beat down the boundaries of my exclusiveness until my sense of separateness is completely enveloped in a sense of fellowship. There must be free and easy access by all, to all the rich resources accumulated by groups and individuals in years of living and experiencing.[150]

For him, the vision for and formation of community - as embodied in the life of Jesus - gives value, structure and purpose to life; it saves life from meaninglessness, frustration, despair, boredom, anxiety and chaos. Community is salvation; it is life at its highest level.[151]   Community (salvation) is not a beyond-this-world hope, but is a possibility for God's love to triumph in history.   Jesus' message of salvation is eschatological in the sense that it pronounces the ability to experience salvation here and now.[152]

Jesus as the Source of Liberation and Hope

Alonzo Johnson, in *Good News for the Disinherited: Howard Thurman on Jesus of Nazareth and Human Liberation,* points out that Jesus came to offer the good news of liberation to the disinherited.[153]   For Howard Thurman, the nature of the church is that it is uniquely and singularly Christological. Teaching, preaching and living the hope that is in Christ have been and continue to be key means of survival amidst the oppressive structures and realities historically incumbent for marginalized (disinherited) persons in the church and society.

The emphasis on Christ as liberator transcends the allegorical and typological approaches to the interpretation of Scripture, and in particular, the interpretation of Jesus of Nazareth.   Thurman's Christological focus undergirds the expectation of spiritual, social and political liberation.

This focus is evident in Jesus' sense of mission and purpose as embodied in the notion of the "liberation" of humanity. Again, this is made clear in the Lukan text:

> The Spirit of the Lord is upon me,
> because he has anointed me

to bring good news to the poor.
He has sent me to proclaim release
to the captives and recovery
of sight to the blind. (Luke 4:18-19)

In this text Jesus essentially outlines his divine purpose, and speaks to the universal nature of the hope that is found in his conception of a liberating ministry with and for all those who are oppressed. Jesus was passionately concerned with the condition of all people, especially the oppressed and disinherited of the earth. He demonstrated this concern by his association with the despised and disinherited persons and groups of his own time.

For Thurman, resurrection hope from a Christian perspective differs from that of mythology insofar as it directs us to the life here on earth in a completely new and, compared to the Old Testament, more incisive fashion. Christians must partake of earthly life to the very end, just as did Christ ("My God, my God, why have you forsaken me?" (Matt. 27:46)), and only by doing so, the Crucified and Resurrected One is with them and they are themselves crucified and resurrected with Christ.

Thurman attested to the critical nature of the life of Jesus as a foundation for comprehending and appropriating Christian hope as a means of moving towards liberation. The message of hope was one that believers in the early church would preach as the cornerstone of the Christian faith. The message of hope - ultimately embodied in the resurrection of Christ - underscores who Jesus was (and is), who in the minds of many followers had entered into salvation history as the embodiment and fulfillment of the messianic promise. The message of hope was one that black slaves in America would sing and preach about, pray to and live for as means of communal and existential survival.[154]

Further, Thurman asserted that Christian faith and hope do not overstep these realities into a heavenly utopia, but seek to address these realities within the context of what he referred to as the "raw materials" of life. It is in following Christ who was raised from suffering, from god-forsaken death and from the grave, that we gain an open prospect in which there is nothing more to oppress people, a view of the realm of liberation and of transformation. The gospel message of Christ calls for personal, communal and systemic liberation and transformation.

Jesus came preaching a message of hope – a hope of peace with justice and righteousness – a radical hope that authentic community could and would be actualized. Amidst the hopelessness, nihilism, despair, oppression and injustice extant in the church and world today – Jesus offers the same hope. In the Jesus of the disinherited, evils like drug addiction and violence, poverty and racism, homophobia and misogyny are addressed, and can be eradicated. Jesus came preaching a message of the hope of a new creation – the hope of radical inclusivity - whereas the prophet Isaiah declared:

> Every valley shall be exalted,
> Every mountain and hill be made low;
> the uneven ground shall become level,
> And the rough places made plain.
> The glory of the Lord shall be revealed,
> And all people shall see it together,
> For the mouth of the Lord has spoken. (Isaiah 40: 4-5)

Concluding Thoughts: Thurman, Jesus and the Church Today

Howard Thurman spoke to the divine and moral imperative that the church shares in seeking to eradicate racial hatred and social disintegration, and advanced the appropriation of the Christian love-ethic as foundational for constructively moving towards the realization of radically inclusive community. He asserted that God's intent is for the human family to live in community as interrelated members. Jesus came into the world to call persons back into community.

Applying Thurman's Christological thought and praxis to the church's life today begins at the point of considering who Jesus was/is as the embodiment of the disinherited. Thurman sums up the identity of Jesus this way:

> Jesus was poor. He was not a Roman citizen like Paul, and was therefore outside the circle of real privilege. He was a carpenter. He did not write a book. He did not travel very far from his home. He was tender without being soft. He was kind without being sentimental. He was gracious without being officious. He refused to be made into a political leader and resisted the pressure to become merely a popular hero.[155]

It is clear that today Jesus would be very concerned about the plight of the very poor and marginalized – the disinherited - in the face of tax reform, healthcare reform, immigration reform, education reform. He said,

> "For I was hungry and you gave me nothing to eat, I was thirsty and you gave me nothing to drink, I was a stranger and you did not invite me in, I needed clothes and you did not clothe me, I was sick and in prison and you did not look after me... whatever you did not do for

one of the least of these, you did not do for me."
(Matthew 25:42-45)

Christian faith does not flee the world, but lives with
hope into the future. To believe in Christ means perpetually
seeking to transcend bounds, and engaging in an ongoing
journey towards liberation and transformation. Yet this happens
in ways that do not seek to suppress or avoid the unpleasant
realities of the world.

In the final analysis, Howard Thurman's Christology,
his explication and appropriation of the identity and ministry of
Jesus, offers insight to the contemporary church, and can be
clearly seen in his co-founding of the Church for the Fellowship
of All Peoples in San Francisco, California in 1944, and in his
lifelong quest for the realization of radically inclusive
community.

CHAPTER FOUR
HOWARD THURMAN, THE CHRISTIAN LOVE-ETHIC
AND THE MOVE TOWARDS A CONCEPTION OF
RADICAL INCLUSUVITY

"Love has no awareness of merit or demerit; it has no scale...
Love loves; this is its nature. Jesus rejected hatred because he
saw that hatred meant death to the mind, death to the spirit,
and death to communion with his Father. He affirmed life;
and hatred was the great denial." - Howard Thurman

Howard Thurman considered the terms "reconciliation" and "love" to be synonymous.[156] He defined love as "the intelligent, kindly but stern expression of kinship of one individual for another, having as its purpose the maintenance and furtherance of life at its highest level."[157] Love responds to an individual's basic need of being cared for. It participates in the attempt to actualize potential, and therefore completes the fragmented and unfulfilled personality. But on a larger scale, love brings together separated lives. It makes apparent the significance of relationships by stressing how inter-dependence is inherent in all of life. Love creates community.[158]

Regarding reconciliation, Thurman wrote, "The quality of reconciliation is that of wholeness; to seek to effect and further harmonize relations in a totally comprehensive climate. The concern for reconciliation finds expression in the simple human desire to understand others and to be understood by others."[159]

Thurman's views on reconciliation are the culmination of several key areas of inquiry. Those universal and transcendent characteristics of life, rooted in relationship with

God as Creator and Sustainer, find their natural manifestation in the yearning for the unity of body, mind and spirit. As Thurman explored reconciliation as a spiritual discipline, he highlighted not only the search for unity in a broken humanity, but also the desire to remedy the lack of harmony within the individual. All this, as he stated, seeks out a state of wholeness which is the natural state of life as intended in the creation.[160] He affirmed this concept in this excerpt from his work, *The Search For Common Ground,* "the man who seeks community with his own spirit, who searches for it in his experiences with the literal facts of the external world, who makes this his formal intent as he seeks to bring order out of the chaos of his collective life, is not going against life but will be sustained and supported by life."[161]

Thurman, Spirituality and the Christian Love-ethic

For Thurman, there was no possibility of radically inclusive community without careful and constructive attention to the *disinherited.* In *Disciplines of the Spirit,* he explained the relationship of the Christian love-ethic to the spiritual quest for wholeness.[162] He characterized the will to segregate and the corollary maltreatment of the disinherited as spiritual problems, and therefore only spiritual answers which affirm the binding attributes of love will suffice. Violence is the act through which the nonexistence of the other person is willed, with hate as the dynamic. At the same time this is an act of self-affirmation, for hate becomes a person's way of saying that they are present. Ultimately, the human spirit cannot tolerate this because it denies the elemental truth of life that "men are made for each other." Violence is in opposition to the "fact of the underlying unity of life." Violence is in opposition to full community.[163]

After a careful consideration of the common need of all humanity to be cared for, Thurman linked nonviolence to the seeking of reconciliation or the state of wholeness which he perceived to be not only a corporate but an individual journey. His development of the basis for the nonviolent act in response to an act of violence is, indeed, as piercing as it is extraordinary. In the course of this discussion, Thurman extends the need to be cared for to the perpetrator of the violence itself, concluding that, in the nonviolent response of the victim; the aggressor is "thrown back upon the naked hunger of his own heart to be cared for."[164] The implications of this line of reasoning are quite dramatic, necessitating a sense of courage on the part of the victim which is far beyond that required to initiate a violent reaction. It is this response in the sheer courage of nonviolence which neutralizes the effect of the violent act, causing hatred to break down for lack of a mechanism by which to be amplified.

It is the cessation of hatred which is at the core of reconciliation both individually and in community. In *Disciplines of the Spirit,* Thurman articulates the grounding language of this concept, "because nonviolence is an affirmation of the existence of the person of violent deeds, in contradistinction to the fact that violence embodies a will to nonexistence, the moral impact which nonviolence carries may potentially realize itself in a given situation by rendering the violent act ineffective and bring about the profoundest kind of change in attitude."[165] His concept of the striving for reconciliation in the human community was not without practical manifestations. His perspectives on reconciliation press towards the acknowledgement of a dedication to realizing the possibilities for productive and fulfilling interaction in the human community.

The experience of crisis is also a necessary aspect of growth both in a physical and spiritual sense for Thurman. Just as there is a tension between the exploration of the unknown and the uncertain, and the desire to remain in the familiar and comfortable in the physical realm, there is a parallel tension associated with spiritual growth. The resolution of this tension resides in the choices made in response to the call for change. A decision to resist change, nevertheless, is a choice which has associated consequences. For Thurman, life presents a series of uniquely patterned crises and resolutions all contributing to the formation of character. [166]

The inescapable aspect of growth, emerging from the need for self-awareness, and the tension of crisis necessitating the rendering of decisions, carry with them an inherent risk. According to Thurman, "growth always involves the risk of failure to fulfill what is implicit in a particular life, its potential." Whenever a choice is made, there is the possibility, or, perhaps the probability of failure in some measure. Citing the Parable of the Talents, however, Thurman makes it clear that refraining from action in the midst of crisis is still a choice, one which may entail the gravest consequences. The aspect of growth in wisdom and stature as it relates to spiritual development can, perhaps, be summarized in Thurman's sentiment, "the discipline of growth becomes the discipline of the spirit, and the increase in stature and wisdom can mean a growth in the knowledge of God and the understanding of His Kingdom."[167]

According to Thurman, much growth is possible through prayer. With regard to prayer, Thurman stated:

> Prayer is a form of communication between God and man, and man and God. It is the essence of

communication between persons that they shall talk with each other from the same agenda. Wherever this is not done, communication tends to break down. If however, an atmosphere of trust can be maintained, then one learns to wait and be still.[168]

Thurman further stated:

The experience of prayer... can be nurtured and cultivated. It can create a climate in which a man's life moves and functions. Indeed, it may become a way of living for the individual. It is ever possible that the time may come when a man carries such an atmosphere around him and gives its quality to all that he does and communicates its spirit to all who cross his path.[169]

In prayer, we discover that the love we are looking for has already been given to us and that we can come to an experience of that love. Prayer is entering into communion with God who molded our being in love. Thurman asserted that "prayer is the experience of the individual as they seek to make the hunger (for God) dominant and controlling in their life. It has to move more and more to the central place until it becomes a conscious and activity of the spirit."[170] Prayer is essentially the act of returning to God. It is the basis of all community-building precisely because in prayer we come to the realization that we do not belong to the world in which conflicts and wars take place, but to God who desires peace and offers us peace. The paradox of community-building is indeed that we seek peace in the world even as we sense that we are not anchored in the world.

Jesus, the Disinherited and the Christian Love-ethic

Historian Lerone Bennett asserts that *Jesus and the Disinherited* offers perhaps the most comprehensive analysis of the Christian love-ethic.[171]   Bennett further suggests that Thurman had a great influence on Martin Luther King, Jr. and his thinking on the Christian love-ethic. When Bennett went to Montgomery, Alabama, shortly after the beginning of the Montgomery Bus Boycott, he was not at all surprised to find King reading not Mohandas Gandhi, but Howard Thurman. In his book, *America's Original Sin: Racism, White Privilege and the Bridge to a New America,* Jim Wallis points out that one of the books that King carried with him whenever he traveled was Thurman's *Jesus and the Disinherited.[172]*

Author and activist, Vincent Harding, recalls that Thurman's *Jesus and the Disinherited* was used by leaders in the civil rights movement as a theological foundation for their activism. They would regularly study and discuss the book together. It provided crucial instruction on nonviolence and the love-ethic as a Christian means for overcoming social oppression. The leaders could better understand how to define and maintain their religious identity in the midst of political struggles.[173] Harding believes that this text defined the spiritual issues related to social transformation, and that it inspired and emboldened leaders as they engaged in the struggle for justice.

In *Jesus and the Disinherited,* Howard Thurman asserted that Jesus was acutely aware of the cultural context of his ministry.[174] Jesus knew that his teachings regarding God's justice, love, mercy, forgiveness and peace would cause controversy and get him into trouble with the religious and political authorities of his day. Yet, he remained faithful to his mission, and sought to perpetually live the God-inspired message that he had been given.

In *Jesus and the Disinherited,* Thurman explored the issue of inclusion within the context of exclusion, and within the context of those denied a rightful place in human society. He reflected that, "The awareness of being a child of God tends to stabilize the ego and results in a new courage, fearlessness and power... Such a man realizes that death cannot possibly be the worst thing in the world. There are some things that are worse than death. To deny one's own integrity of personality in the presence of human challenge is one of those things."[175] Certainly, sharing his Grandmother Nancy Ambrose's stories of identity as a child of God affirmed the vital worth of spiritual self-awareness for Thurman.

Clearly, Thurman's conception of Christian love was rooted in the example of the unconditional love of Christ. The practice of unconditional love is essential to the breaking down of social barriers such as racism. As early as 1928 in his article, "Peace Tactics and a Racial Minority," Thurman began to outline how a "philosophy of pacifism" can begin to eliminate whites' will to control, and blacks' will to hate. His primary concern was to call a truce to attitudes which promote separation.[176]

Thurman understood racism and other forms of bigotry to be contradictions of life.[177] He stated that "A bigot is a person who makes an idol of his commitments." George D. Kelsey, in *Racism and the Christian Understanding of Man,* similarly intimated that "Racism is a faith. It is a form of idolatry. It is an abortive search for meaning."[178] Indeed, racism is inimical to the formation of identity and community. Neither blacks nor whites can attain a proper sense of self and give full expression to their potential in an environment of prejudice, segregation and violence. Systematic discrimination sabotages the function of community as a place of nurture and growth through cooperation. Destructive forces are released to rupture life's inter-relatedness.

Thurman shared a story of a dog who had been constantly threatened by children in its neighborhood. Walking down the street, it would growl at any child playing outside. The children in response would cock their arms as if to throw rocks at the dog. Both reactions derived from fear - the dog's fear of being struck, and the children's fear of being bitten.

Metaphysically, hate and love cannot coexist. Love emerges in the striving towards contact that pushes against the things that divide humanity. Hate is bred by fear of "difference" and is a by-product of a will to divide. Hatred today is a societal contagion that manifests itself in various forms of racism, classism, sexism, misogyny, homophobia, xenophobia, Islamophobia and anti-immigration.

Racism continues to be America's preeminent form of hatred. *It is the elephant in the nation's living room.* It is real and it is pervasive in American society and the church today, and it, along with class/classism and gender/sexism, plays a significant role in everything that occurs socio-politically in America. Those who continue to deny racism's existence and pervasiveness, or try to wish it away are merely prolonging the wait for a real opportunity for the society and churches to (really) heal and move forward into real forms of inclusivity, equality and justice.

The Christian Love-ethic and the Striving toward Community

For Thurman, love is the expression of the theological concept of related "being," and is the context for all relationships of Christian nurture. It was love for one another, Jesus said, that identified his disciples to the world (John

13:35). This was to be ultimately expressed in the ability to love one's enemy (Matthew 5:43).

Regarding love of one's enemy, Thurman stated:

Love of the enemy means a fundamental attack must first be made on the enemy status. How can this be done? Does it mean ignoring the fact that he belongs to the enemy class? Hardly. For lack of a better term, an "unscrambling" process is required. Obviously a situation has to be set up in which it is possible for primary contacts to be multiplied. By this I do not mean contacts that are determined by status or by social distinctions. There are always primary contacts between the weak and the strong, the privileged and the underprivileged, but they are generally contacts within zones of agreement, which leave the status of the individual intact. There is a great intimacy between whites and Negroes, but it is usually between servant and served, between employer and employee. Once the status of each is frozen or fixed, contacts are merely truces between enemies – a kind of armistice for purposes of economic security.[179]

Grounded in and shaped by the vicissitudinous struggles of black America, Thurman offered a perspective on the universal phenomenon of religiously-related social change among oppressed and exploited peoples that is at once accordant and distinctive. The capacity of African Americans to decry the debasements of the larger society through a plethora of means – often discernibly religious in promotion, both violent and non-violent in expression – is historic, deep-rooted and not without considerable documentation.[180]

It is a well-known fact that the condition of struggle is not restricted to the North American context, but has numerous counterparts wherever situations of cross-cultural contact – that is, Western forms of conquest and domination – have occurred in the modern world in various settings. A canvassing of literature in this area reveals a strong bond of commonality among these seemingly disparate movements, not infrequently reflected in their mystic-like envisagement or cognition of a regenerate and reordered society, where the value of all human life and the actualizing of human potential is ascendant. Thus, at least in their initial stages, a holistic sense of re-creation and affirmation with respect to self, community, and culture is often found to inform and permeate movements in the "Two-Thirds World."[181]

Luther Smith argues that Thurman did more than any other person to articulate the ethical and spiritual necessity for blacks' civil liberties struggle to be grounded in the principles of nonviolence. Thurman suggested that nonviolent resistance and protests (i.e. boycotts, non-cooperation, demonstrations, sit-ins) were key means of providing shock and transforming the social order. The development of a philosophy of nonviolent protest in the black struggle is a foremost achievement of social witness. Here, he made a signal contribution to providing a peaceful method for change in American race relations.

Thurman began to outline more fully the basic principles of his philosophy of nonviolence, the Christian love-ethic and radically inclusive community in the early part of 1935 at the annual convocation on preaching at the School of Theology of Boston University. This material was later developed into the book *Jesus and the Disinherited.*[182] For Thurman, the loving community of peace, justice and equality can only be attained by nonviolent and loving means. Community cannot be built on the tools of hatred. Nonviolence responds in a caring way to the perpetrator of violence. It insists that the well-being of the individuals involved is of ultimate concern. It moves the level of confrontation to a higher spiritual plane. Instead of merely defeating one's offender physically or psychologically, one begins to create the climate for love to be a force, which has to be dealt with within the context of relationships and fellowship. The presence of loving care introduces new possibilities for reconciliation. Only nonviolence permits love to enter conflict creatively and address the prevailing spiritual ills of separation, fear and hatred.

Howard Thurman and Quest for Beloved Community

In the final analysis, what Howard Thurman, and later Martin Luther King, Jr. advocated for when they spoke of the Christian love-ethic was the *Beloved Community*. The *Beloved Community* is not something that is passive, weak and anemic but is a loving community that is vibrant, and in many ways can be revolutionary and counter cultural, tough love. [183]

In Thurman's work, along with that of the likes of King, Josiah Royce and others, several features of the *Beloved Community* can be identified. First, the *Beloved Community* is rooted in the biblical notion of agape love (God's unconditional love), and is the ultimate goal for the world (creation). It, according to King, is the love of God operating in the human heart, and seeks to "preserve and create community." Second, the *Beloved Community* recognizes and honors the image of God in every human being. It understands everybody as somebody, and offers radical hospitality to everyone, as a part of an inclusive family, the world house. It exhibits true respect and validation of others. Third, the *Beloved Community* seeks peace with justice, righteously opposes oppression and injustice, and takes direct action against racism, poverty and violence. True peace is always connected with justice. King stated that "true peace is not merely the absence of tension; it is the presence of justice. Fourth, the *Beloved Community* depends on collaborative efforts of cross-sections of people with common interests for a just society. The sentiments Rabbi Abraham Joshua Heschel resonate, "Morally speaking, there is no limit to the concern one must feel for the suffering of human beings; indifference to evil is worse than evil itself, and in a free society, some are guilty, but all are responsible."[184] Archbishop Desmond Tutu stated that "If you are neutral in situations of injustice, you have chosen the side of the oppressor." Similarly, German theologian Dietrich Bonhoeffer intimated that (for all of us), "not to speak is to speak is to speak, and not to act is to act."[185] Fifth and finally, the *Beloved Community* affirms that all of humanity is an inescapable network of mutuality among the human family. King intimated that "all life is interrelated." One of his fundamental beliefs was in the kinship of all persons. He believed that all of life is part of a single process; all living things are interrelated; and all persons are sisters and brothers. All of us have a place in the *Beloved Community*. Because all of us are interrelated, one cannot harm another without harming oneself. King elaborated:

> To the degree that I harm my brother, no matter what he is doing to me, to that extent I am harming myself. For example, white men often refuse federal aid to education in order to avoid giving the Negro his rights; but because all men are brothers, they cannot deny Negro children without harming themselves. Why is this? Because all men are brothers. If you harm me, you harm yourself. Love, *agape*, is the only cement that can hold

this broken community together. When I am commanded to love, I am commanded to restore community, to resist injustice, and to meet the needs of my brothers.[186]

Like King, Thurman shaped his ministry out of the firm conviction that "all life is interrelated." But somewhat unlike King, Thurman was not primarily interested in exposing America's racial sins before the world community; nor did Thurman spend a great deal of time making impassioned appeals to the moral conscience of the nation, seeking to remind the church and the government of their Christian and democratic principles.

Thurman sought to demonstrate human interrelatedness, and test the capacity to build radically inclusive community primarily through the practice of religious experience. In this regard, Thurman sought to be more intentionally multicultural than King in his practice of the radically inclusive religious community. In his pastoral work in Ohio and San Francisco, and in his teaching and campus ministries at Howard and Boston universities, Thurman experimented with creative worship styles that would appeal to congregants from diverse cultural, religious, social and ethnic backgrounds. Essentially, he believed that authentic religious experience transcends "all superficial categories that separate and divide people and allows them to sense their relatedness to all humanity."

He felt that a key vehicle for effecting constructive change was nonviolence, not necessarily as employed by movement leaders – Martin Luther King, Jr. being a conspicuous exception – but a more involved commitment to nonviolence as personal, spiritual discipline and technique. Thurman cast nonviolence as a creative, ethical approach to change, capable of producing specific ramifications in individuals and society. [187] Thurman asserted that the effect of nonviolence on the offender is apt to be so threatening that the security they feel in the violent act deserts them and they are thrown back upon the naked hunger of their own heart to be cared for, to be understood, to experience themselves in harmony with their fellows.[188]

The importance of both factors must not, however, be misconstrued, for as Thurman made manifestly clear, not even nonviolence as a collective device can guarantee social change. Rather, the major contribution of nonviolence is that it creates and maintains a "climate" wherein protagonists may be brought into a single commitment. To paraphrase Thurman, nonviolence affirms the existence of the "other," however defined, whereas violence embodies a will to non-existence which, translated at the level of society, means non-community. This affirmation of the existence of the "other", in essence, is the nature of the *Beloved Community*.

Thurman and a Philosophy of Nonviolence

Luther Smith asserts that contrary to most public perceptions, it was Howard Thurman's conception of community that served as the primary philosophic foundation for the Civil Rights movement of the 1950s and 1960s.[189] According to Smith, Thurman's concept of community tied the black struggle for freedom to divine will and destiny. The black struggle then became a holy struggle. In defining the ethic of nonviolence, he gave the freedom movement a holy mechanism. This identification of Thurman as the creative mind behind the development of a philosophy of nonviolence for the black struggle underscores the significant contribution of his social, prophetic witness. The beginning of a philosophy of nonviolence in the civil rights struggle of black America is often traced to Martin Luther King, Jr. and the Montgomery Bus Boycott, which began in 1954. Although the boycott may represent the most successful, notable and visible application of this nonviolent philosophy in America, nonviolence as a means of addressing the American race problem received considerable discussion and shaping beginning in the 1930s through the work of persons like Howard Thurman and Benjamin Mays.[190]

Thurman understood nonviolence to be the only Christian means of struggle validated in Scripture. Indeed, for him and other black religious thinkers prior to the emergence of the Black Power movement and the advent of Black liberation theology of the late 1960s, the praxis of Jesus and the Christian love-ethic were the authoritative sources for Christian living in the area of race relations and building radically inclusive community. Therefore, Thurman rejected hatred, bitterness, and violence as acceptable Christian behavior. For him, nonviolence was the only way Christians could be true to the love-ethic of Jesus. These views are expressed throughout his writings, and can also be found in the writings of persons like Benjamin Mays, George Kelsey and Martin Luther King, Jr.

While Thurman was clearly influenced by the thinking of Mohandas Gandhi, and gleaned a great deal from social critics such as Henry David Thoreau and A.J. Muste, from long-time social activists like Bayard Rustin and Glenn Smiley, and from Jesus' Sermon on the Mount in the New Testament (Matthew 5-7), it is critical to understand their/these respective concepts of nonviolence in relation to the southern black Christian tradition.[191] Thurman was also profoundly impacted by black Christian leaders like Mordecai Johnson and Benjamin Mays whose traditional forms of nonviolence had long represented moderation in the midst of the violence of white

America. Thurman's decision to embrace nonviolence in its personal, spiritual, social and ethical dimensions resulted more from his experiences with the practical applications of the method of nonviolence among black southerners than from any other intellectual or spiritual source.

Thurman often pointed to the strength and leadership of historic black figures like Frederick Douglass, Harriet Tubman, Booker T. Washington, and W.E.B. Dubois to show that a tradition of nonviolence and the Christian love-ethic – rooted in the black church - has shaped the ongoing praxis of nonviolence as a means of resistance, survival, actualization, peace and community-building for marginalized persons in America.

Thurman viewed the challenge to act nonviolently as one of the most formidable challenges facing the church and society on the brink of the new age. For him, nonviolence, through the appropriation of the Christian love-ethic, was critical to the realization of radically inclusive community.

This means that the Christian virtues of love, mercy, justice and forgiveness should stand at the center of our lives. Like Mohandas Gandhi, Thurman intimated that there is the danger that those who have lived for prolonged periods under the yoke of oppression, those who have been exploited and trampled over, those who have had to stand amidst the tragedies of injustice and indignities will enter the new age with hate and bitterness. But he argued that to retaliate with hate and bitterness, would mean that the new age will be nothing but a duplication of the old age.

Underlying his thinking on love, reconciliation and nonviolence was Thurman's firm belief in the power of Christianity – the teachings of Jesus of Nazareth - to transform lives. Thurman interpreted Jesus's teachings on forgiveness, reconciliation and love of one's enemies quite literally, pointing out that Christian nonviolence is an act of profound love that seeks to redeem oppressors, not to humiliate or destroy them.

He synthesized his treatment of Christian love by referring to the need to forgive the enemy for injury. He contended that in the insistence of Jesus that persons develop the capacity to forgive seventy times seven (Matthew 18:22), there seemed to be the assumption that forgiveness is mandatory for three reasons: (1) God forgives us again and again for what we do intentionally and unintentionally; (2) no evil deed represents the full intention of the person; (3) and the evil doer will be punished.[192] In the wide sweep of the ebb and flow of moral law, our deeds track us down, and doer and deed meet.[193]

In addition to the teachings of the Christian scriptures, Thurman noted that nonviolence was rooted in the history of the black American experience of protest and resistance dating back to slavery. He contended that the Negro spirituals were a critical source of resistance, and were to be understood as critical means of nonviolent protest and sources of strength in the praxis of the Christian love-ethic over the ages.[194] The spirituals are not songs of hate, revenge or conquest, but rather songs of the soul that helped slaves survive and protest oppression without bitterness and violence.[195] James Cone elaborates on Thurman's perspective on the Negro spirituals as a source of protest, empowerment and means of moving towards freedom:

> Howard Thurman was one of the first scholars to use religion as the starting point in his interpretation of the black spirituals. According to Thurman, "The clue to the meaning of the spirituals is to be found in religious experience and spiritual discernment." In the spirituals, he perceives "the elemental and formless struggle to a vast consciousness in the mind and spirit of the

individual." According to Thurman, the black spiritual
is an expression of the slave's determination to *be* in a
society that seeks to destroy their personhood. It is an
affirmation of the dignity of the black slaves, the
essence of humanity of their spirits. Where human life
is regarded as property and death has no dignity, "the
human spirit is stripped to the literal substance of itself."
Deprived of power, the slaves found ways to hold
together their personhood. To be sure, the insights
reflected in the slaves' struggle for being may not have
been original, but, in the presence of the naked demand
upon the primary sources of meanings, even without
highly specialized tools or skills, the universe
responded... with overwhelming power.[196]

Thus, for Thurman, spirituals like "We are Climbing
Jacob's Ladder," and "Swing Low, Sweet Chariot," and "Go
Down Moses, and later songs like "We Shall Overcome" which
became the "anthem" of the Civil Rights movement, were to be
understood within the context of nonviolent protest and the
historic quest for freedom and radically inclusive community.[197]

Thurman's progressive and insightful interpretation of
the Negro Spirituals as a source for doing theology, coupled
with his appropriation of themes of the black religious tradition
served as a spiritual and intellectual model for Martin Luther
King, Jr. and other leaders of the Civil Rights movement. King
did not focus a great deal in his writing and speaking on
"spirituality" - as it is generally understood - as a means of
constructively developing the *Beloved Community*. He spoke
more to the problem of racism in its moral, ethical and socio-
cultural dimensions than did Thurman. Both, Thurman and
King, however, took every opportunity to show how the

historical experiences of African Americans, particularly their religious experiences, spoke to the prevailing situation in American life, and how these religious experiences could thus serve as an impetus to building radically inclusive community.

Thurman was not averse to nonviolent social action and protest as a means of moving persons toward a more profound sense of community and away from what he referred to as the "will to segregate."[198] With regard to this, Thurman said:

What do I do then? I may resort to the exercise of some form of shock by organizing a boycott, or widespread noncooperation, or the like. The function of these techniques is to tear people free from their alignments to the evil way, to free them so that they may be given an immediate sense of acute insecurity and out of the depths of their insecurity be forces to see their kinship with the weak and the insecure. People do not voluntarily relinquish their hold on their place. It is not until something becomes movable in the situation that they are spiritually prepared to apply Christian idealism to un-ideal and unchristian situations. Examples of these techniques are being developed by (groups) in different parts of the world even now. Action of this kind requires great discipline of mind, emotions, and body to the end that forces may not be released that will do complete violence both to one's ideals and one's purpose. All must be done with the full consciousness of the Divine Scrutiny.[199]

In reflecting on the ways that Thurman talked and wrote about the context in which Jesus lived out His love-ethic, it is difficult not to think about how so many of us are challenged today to live out a Christian love-ethic. At one point, Thurman intimated the importance of considering the ethical significance

97

of the religion of Jesus in light of the Zulu proverb: "Full belly child says to empty belly child, be of good cheer." The love-ethic that Thurman proffers has no constrictions in that we are free to respond and react in ways that can lead to greater, contagious forms of love and community among us. The Christian love-ethic allows us to be free to love as Christ loved, and as Christ instructs us to love.

Thurman set forth love that is much more than an emotion or feeling. Love as lived out and taught by Jesus is love that is acted out in ways that are irrespective of whether love is deserved or even reciprocated. It is agape love.

Thurman's insights were put into practice in innovative ministry settings. The Church for the Fellowship of All Peoples in 1944 was the primary case. It was organized as an intentionally interracial, intercultural, interreligious organization which valued diversity of theological expression and life experience. This project became a shining example of the possibility for a truly inclusive faith community which valued all peoples in light of their common humanity and shared relationship with God. His pastoral career was dedicated to programming designed to nurture and cultivate these principles.[200] Thurman clearly saw the potential for humankind to realize the essence of radically inclusive community.

CHAPTER FIVE

FELLOWSHIP CHURCH AND AN EXPERIMENT IN RADICAL INCLUSIVITY

"To be victimized by error and to continue making choices of integrity, is to grow in grace." - Howard Thurman

Howard Thurman's thoughts on the importance of community were rooted in his feelings of being personally victimized by racism. He was acutely aware that racism attacked his self-worth and freedom. It attacked the well-being of community. His mystical experiences, however, provided the assurance that he was a beloved child of God, and that harmonious relatedness is the underlying structure of reality. Racism denied the truth about God's intent for creation. It put the welfare of the community in crisis. Over time, the pastoral-questions for Thurman became: How could he help shape a social reality that conformed to his religious beliefs? How could he speak to the crisis by restoring the community's (especially America's) sense of well-being?[201]

The opportunity to further explore his convictions about the unifying nature of the religious experience came in 1944 when Thurman was invited by the Fellowship of Reconciliation to join Rev. Dr. Alfred G. Fisk (a white Presbyterian minister and college professor) as a co-pastor of a new interracial church in San Francisco. After prayerful consideration, Thurman left his tenured professorship and position as Dean of Andrew Rankin Memorial Chapel at Howard University and ventured westward, excited about the challenges of an interracial ministry. About the decision to go to San Francisco, he stated:

> Here at last I could put to the test once more the major concern of my life. Is the worship of God the central and most significant act of the human spirit? Is it really true that in the presence of God there is neither male or female, child or adult, rich or poor, or any classification by which mankind defines itself in categories, however meaningful?[202]

When the invitation came for Thurman to help organize the Church for the Fellowship of All Peoples in San Francisco, he saw it as an opportunity to realize his Khyber Pass vision.[203] San Francisco, with its cultural diversity, was not a controlled environment and could serve as a true laboratory for Thurman's dream. It was an opportunity to test the power of Christianity to overcome the separateness of discrimination, prejudice and segregation – to test the ability of the Church to be a loving interracial fellowship – to test, as Thurman states, "the future of democracy."[204]

The racial makeup of San Francisco in 1944 made it the ideal location for testing Thurman's fundamental theological concern. Whites, Asian-Americans, Mexican-Americans, Native Americans and African Americans lived side by side during a time of deep ethnic tension. Specifically, the steady arrival of black migrants in search of jobs in the war industries; the white backlash to increased racial diversity; and the relocation of Japanese-Americans to concentration camps, created a social climate that was a potential racial powder keg.[205]

In this environment, Thurman wanted to prove that through authentic religious experience, people could transcend racial barriers and appreciate the interrelatedness of all humanity.[206] The Church for the Fellowship of All Peoples (officially organized in October 1944) developed a program and liturgy especially designed to foster unity in the midst of cultural and religious diversity. Both children and adults were regularly exposed to the contributions of different ethnic groups through worship experiences, forum discussions, lectures, games, recitals, art exhibits, and international dinners. As a result, "slowly there began to emerge a climate in which the fruits of culture could be appreciated, assimilated, and shared without patronage and condescension."[207]

Fellowship and the Movement towards Radically Inclusive Community

The concept behind Thurman's use of the term "fellowship" is explicated by Henry Nelson Wieman. Wieman distinguished "sympathetic" and "instrumental" association from "organic" association. Sympathetic association is defined as "one in which the people associated share the same feelings, the same thoughts, the same aspirations, the same hopes and purposes."[208] Instrumental association is one in which persons work together in order to provide charitable services for others. It is organic association, however, which describes what Thurman meant by "fellowship." [209]

In organic association, possessing the same feelings, thoughts and purpose is not essential. Persons may differ significantly on issues, but through fellowship, develop an appreciation of other perspectives while finding their own nurtured by the contact. Service is not excluded from organic association. Its purpose is to create the environment that makes organic interaction possible. Since, as Thurman believed, the universe is by nature organic, this type of fellowship is the only kind that produces harmonious living. Through organic fellowship inter-relatedness and reconciliation are realized. Organic fellowship is synonymous with Thurman's concept of community.

Thurman criticized the Christian church as a supporter of a limited form of community, and a flawed sense of fellowship. He attributed this mainly to racial separation prevalent in church life, along with the church's zeal to identify the "saved" and the "damned." Separating and categorizing eventually lead certain groups of people to feel morally superior (or inferior) to others. When this mood infiltrates a group, conditions are set for a hostility which only works for limited community.[210] Thurman said:

> It is to the utter condemnation of the church that large groups of believers all over the United States have stood, and, at present, stand on the side of a theory of inequality among men that causes the church to practice in its own body some of the most vicious forms of racial prejudice... The bitter truth is that the church has permitted the various hate-inspired groups in our common life to establish squatter's rights in the minds of believers because there has been no adequate teaching of the meaning of the faith in terms of human dignity and human worth.[211]

Thurman saw what he termed the "will to segregate" as the primary hindrance to the development of fellowship and inclusive community in the church and society.[212] The "will to segregate," Thurman said, "has taken the form of policy in business, in the church, in the state, in the school, in living zones." Thurman asserted that the church's task with regard to overcoming this "will to segregate" would be to engage in a radical reorganization of policy and structural change. Thurman said:

> I am realistic enough to know that this cannot be done overnight. My contention is that if the "will to segregate" is relaxed in the church, then the resources of mind and spirit and power that are already in the church can begin working formally and informally in the radical changes that are necessary if the church is to become Christian. This, of course, may not mean that there will be no congregations that are all Negro or that are all white, but freedom of choice, which is basically a sense of alternatives, will be available to any persons without regard to the faithful perpetuation of the pattern of segregation upon which the Christian church in America is constructed.[213]

For Thurman, the Christian church has the potential for modeling radically inclusive community. He believed that churches had too often been formed out of an ethos of segregation and exclusion. Churches typically excluded those who did not believe specific dogmas, and also excluded those who believed the accepted dogma, but who were of a certain socio-economic status or cultural background.[214] He believed that as long as the church operated on the principle of exclusion, it could not faithfully be the fully actualized trustee of religious experience and radically inclusive community.

Since community is ideally formed and nourished by the Christian love-ethic, opportunities must therefore be established for people to be in organic fellowship in order to express love and to be loved. Thurman asserted:

> It is necessary, therefore, for the privileged and the underprivileged to work on the common environment

for the purpose of providing normal experiences of fellowship. This is one very important reason for the insistence that segregation is a complete ethical and moral evil. Whatever it may do for those who dwell on either side of the wall, one thing is certain: it poisons all normal contacts for those persons involved. The first step toward love is a common sharing of a sense of mutual worth and value.[215]

In *The Search for Common Ground,* Thurman anticipated new opportunities to experience radically inclusive community when he wrote:

It is time for assessing and reassessing resources in the light of the most ancient memory of the race concerning community, to hear again the clear voice of prophet and seer calling for harmony among all the children of men. At length there will begin to be talk of plans for the new city – that has never before existed on land or sea.[216]

Thurman continued to articulate his vision for organic fellowship by saying:

One day there will stand up in their midst one who will tell of a new sickness among the children who in their delirium cry for their brothers whom they have never known and from whom they have been cut off behind the self-imposed barriers of their fathers. An alarm will spread throughout the community that it is being felt and slowly realized that community cannot feed for long on itself; it can only flourish where always the boundaries are giving way to the coming of others from beyond them – unknown and undiscovered brothers. [217]

Fellowship Church and the Living of Radical Inclusivity

Thurman's concept of the striving for fellowship and unity in the human community was not without practical manifestations. His entire ministry was dedicated to realizing the possibilities for productive and fulfilling interaction in the human community. He clearly saw the potential for humankind to realize the essence of reconciliation and fellowship.

His inclination was put into practice in unique ministry settings, with the Church for the Fellowship of All Peoples being one such model. It valued diversity of theological expression and life experience, and it became a shining example of the possibility for a truly inclusive faith community which valued all peoples in light of their creation by God, and their relationship with God. Thurman's pastoral ministry throughout his career was dedicated to programming designed to nurture and cultivate these principles.[218]

At Fellowship Church, diverse persons participated as equals in developing the church as it sought to model racial, and other forms of social harmony. Thurman noted that until his departure from Fellowship Church in 1953, 60 percent of the membership was Caucasian, 35 percent were Negroes, and 5 percent were from other ethnic groups such as Mexican-American, Asian-American and Native American. There was also a broad range of educational levels in the congregation.[219] In addition to racial and cultural heterogeneity, the church represented a broad cross-section of the religious spectrum: Quaker, Baptist, Roman Catholic, Presbyterian, Jewish, Congregational, Methodist and Episcopal, but also those who held no particular (religious) affinity.[220]

In his book, *Footprints of a Dream*, Thurman described the organizing, programming, worship and fellowship of the church. He stated that Fellowship Church's significance was not just in its ability to bring together separate groups, but in the quality of religious experiences and the life-changing effects that those experiences provided individuals. The church created, through its worship and fellowship, opportunities for persons to have a proper sense of self and the urge to establish community.[221] He stated, "We were convinced that a way could be found to create a religious fellowship worthy of transcending racial, cultural, and social distinctions."[222] In his estimation, for a moment in time, Fellowship Church was able to celebrate their diversity and achieve a state of being which, was the essence of inclusive fellowship.

Fellowship Church's principles and values toward radically inclusive community are articulated in its membership statement, "The Commitment":

> I affirm my need for a growing understanding of all people as children of God and I seek after a vital experience of God as revealed through Jesus of Nazareth and other great religious spirits whose fellowship with God was the foundation of their fellowship with all people.
>
> I desire to share in the spiritual growth and ethical awareness of men and women of varied national, cultural, racial, and creedal heritage united in a religious fellowship.
>
> I desire the strength of corporate worship through membership in The Church for the Fellowship of All Peoples with the imperative of personal dedication to the working out of God's purpose here and in all places.[223]

Thurman sought to move persons – across cultures – toward community defined by relationships rather than accomplishment. He called for new attitudes as well as new achievements, new partnerships as well as new prosperity, and he saw the need for interracial, intercultural and interclass cooperation that reflected a healthy respect for persons and a commitment to work on their behalf. In addition, Fellowship Church cultivated an openness to religious truth beyond the confines of Judeo-Christian thought. The members expressed their ecumenical, interfaith attitude in the spirit of Galatians 3:28:

> It is our faith that in the presence of God - with His dream of order – there is neither male nor female; white nor black, Gentile nor Jew; Protestant nor Catholic; Hindu nor Buddhist nor Moslem – but a human spirit, stripped to the literal substance of itself.[224]

Again, Thurman's ecclesiology for social change was not to organize Fellowship Church as the base to spearhead a mass social movement. Instead, he placed importance on empowering the individual to live responsibly in whatever situations she or he works, socializes, recreates or serves. For him, Fellowship Church was primarily a religious, and not merely a social experiment. This is evident in his statement, "The experience of worship became the keystone of the entire structure. My basic concern was the deepening of the spiritual life of the gathered people."[225]

Throughout the descriptions of his work at Fellowship Church, there is the emphasis on the development of the religious idiom that enabled people from various religious (and non-religious) traditions to have a common experience of God's loving presence. Again, Thurman's ecclesiology did not necessarily call for the involvement of Fellowship Church (as an institution) in the politics of society, but aimed primarily at empowering individuals spiritually to address economic, political and social needs as an outgrowth of religious experience. Thurman wrote:

> The core of my preaching has always concerned itself with the development of the inner resources needed for the creation of a friendly world of friendly men... It was my conviction and determination that the church would be a resource for activists – a mission fundamentally perceived. To me it was important that individuals who were in the thick of the struggle for social change would be able to find renewal and fresh courage in the spiritual resources of the church.[226]

Fellowship Church received national acclaim for its example in race relations, and radical inclusivity. The church became a model of possibility for churches nonplussed and paralyzed by social diversity. It became a model of Christian witness for a pluralistic society. Through Fellowship Church, Howard Thurman and Albert Fisk proved the inclusive genius of Christianity. The church provided the empirical evidence Thurman needed to confirm the insights from his own mystical consciousness about life's teleological concern for community. The experiment of Fellowship Church verified the ability of Christianity and its institutions to be conduits that are capable of exposing and effectively addressing major contradictions of life, especially racism, and other forms of segregation.

In the tradition of the Hebrew prophets and within the context of the prophetic pastoral option, Howard Thurman called on America and the Christian church to recall the sources of their identity; for America the *Declaration of Independence and Constitution,* and for Christianity the inclusive love-ethic as taught by Jesus. The Church for the Fellowship of All Peoples sought to embody these resources.

Fellowship Church became a shining example of the possibility for a truly radically inclusive faith community which valued all peoples. Fellowship Church to this day credits its diversity to "the extraordinary heritage of Thurman's penetrating theology, articulated in over a dozen books."[227] In his nine year experience with Fellowship Church (1944-53), Thurman clearly saw and demonstrated the potential for humanity to realize the essence of reconciliation through radical inclusivity.

CHAPTER SIX

HOWARD THURMAN AND THE QUEST FOR COMMON GROUND

"When you can go deep down inside yourself, really know who you are and are secure in who you are—then—you can find yourself in every other human being."
- Howard Thurman

Thurman and a Vision of Common Ground

Howard Thurman was among those who spoke to the divine and moral imperative to move towards harmonious unity that Christians must share in seeking common ground and the common good. This imperative – this calling - is rooted and grounded in a divine commitment to advance the appropriation of the Christian love-ethic as foundational for constructively moving towards the realization of radically inclusive community and the common good. Thurman asserted that God's intent is for the human family to live in community as interrelated members. Jesus came into the world to call persons back into community.

Much of what was articulated, and in-fact appropriated as the common good through the middle of the 20th century has been obscured at the least, and at worst has been lost and forgotten as we've moved into the 21st century. Perhaps as a reflection of society in general, churches today seem to have become more inwardly focused; religion and faith have become increasingly privatized and insular. As a result, forms of external religious expression like ecumenism, interreligious and interfaith dialogue and engagement, and the capacity of churches to critically engage culture and society in the public square have, in large measure, been diminished.

110

An imitation of the unconditional love revealed in the life and teachings of Jesus can be helpful in the quest for common ground and the common good today. Moving toward a deeper sense of who we are as individuals and community enables us to live more shalom-filled lives, modeled on the life of Christ. There is the obligation to treat every person as Christ Himself, respecting her/his life as if it were the life of Christ.

Thurman's earliest experiences of community and non-community in the segregated South had a profound impact on his quest for and interpretation of human community, and thus his quest for a comprehension and appropriation of common ground. Again, Walter Fluker suggests that the experiential and intellectual sources of the ideal of community in Thurman demonstrate that his understanding of community arose initially from the experience of oppression and segregation in the Deep South.[228] Those early experiences, and later ones, are given in autobiographical statements throughout his writings, sermons and speeches.

Thurman's book, *The Search for Common Ground,* is devoted to verifying the principle of the unity of life and common ground, by examining the creation myths of culture, the life sciences, the philosophy behind utopias, and the social psychology of change in America as means of identifying and nurturing commonality among persons from diverse backgrounds. Thurman believed that the urge for and movement towards community, toward harmonious unity in life, could be found everywhere from the smallest cell to the whole universe.[229]

Out of the particularity of these experiences emerged a universal vision of human community which transcended race, class, religion and other forms of sectarianism. His early childhood experiences in the contexts of family, the black church, and the black communities of Daytona Beach, Florida provided Thurman with a sense of personal worth and an awareness of the interrelatedness of life which became central elements in his views of community.[230]

Thurman's quest for harmonious unity is characterized by its ability to allow persons (and nature) to actualize their potential. In actualizing potential, persons come to recognize and realize their worth and purpose in life.[231]

Thurman affirmed the centrality of personality in forming a sense of community. He believed that community results from a sense of unity with life (inter- and intra-relatedness). This is only possible if the individual has a sense of "self" (inner-relatedness). The development of his theology begins with the individual. He believed that the individual personality is of infinite worth, and that its significance and nurture are essential concerns of religion. In understanding the principles that affirm, sustain and give meaning to the individual, one has the key to understanding that which affirms, sustains and gives meaning to community and ultimately to the universe.[232]

For Thurman, two matters are essential for a true sense of self. First, since a person's inherent worth is of ultimate value, it is important that one's self-image conforms to one's own sense of reality. He was convinced that an accurate sense of self is the only "basis that the dignity of man, the individual, can be restored."[233] Secondly, though one's sense of reality is inherent, the nurture of this reality towards a healthy self-image is a social function. Thurman says, "We are all related either positively or negatively to some immediate social unit, which provides the other-than-self reference that in turn undergirds the sense of self. Such a primary group confers *persona* upon the individual; it fashions and fortifies the character structure."[234]

In shaping his ministry out of the belief that all life is interrelated, Thurman believed that nations, ethnic groups and religious communities inhibit the realization of human community when they emphasize the differences that separate people instead of the common ties that bind them together.[235] Thurman captured the essence of his perspective on human interrelatedness:

> To experience oneself as a human being is to feel life moving through one and claiming one as a part of it...It is not the experience of oneself as male or female, as black or white, as American or European. It is rather the experience of oneself as being. It is at such a time that one can hear the sound of the genuine in other human beings.[236]

For Thurman, the conception of the inherent dignity and worth of all human beings developed very early out of his experience in the black family and church. His parents' and grandparents' teachings on the sacredness of humanity were reinforced by what he heard in church concerning the Judeo-Christian view of humanity being created in the image of God. This concept of *imago dei* in the black church developed out of a heritage of the slaves, who despite their (relatively) untutored state, caught the significance of the fact that every human soul is a part of God and is therefore dear to the heart of God.[237]

The basic principle behind his concept of community was that "the literal fact of the underlying unity of life seems to be established beyond doubt." He developed this principle in saying:

> If life has been fashioned out of a fundamental unity and ground, and if it has developed within a structure, then it is not to be wondered at that the interest in and concern

for wholeness should be part of the conscious intent of life, more basic than any particular conscious tendency toward fragmentation… It (reconciliation) seeks to effect and further harmonize relations in a totally comprehensive climate.[238]

The vision of community gives value, structure and purpose to life; it saves life from meaninglessness, frustration, despair, boredom, anxiety and chaos. Community is salvation; it is life at its highest level.[239]   For Thurman, community (salvation) is not a beyond-this-world hope, but is a possibility for God's love to triumph in history.   Jesus' message of salvation is eschatological in the sense that it pronounces the ability to experience salvation here and now.[240]

A Framework for Common Ground in the 21st Century
Howard Thurman saw the problem of an excluding church as being rooted in the fact that too many Christians have not clearly understood or faithfully followed the central personality of the faith, Jesus the Christ. Thurman insisted that community brings ultimate meaning to life. He also intimated that "community as it is experienced in the far-flung hopes of persons in all ages finds its greatest fulfillment in a picture of what the collective life of humanity would be like if it functioned in keeping with humanity's high destiny."[241]
The quest for common ground, and by extension, the common good is at the heart of the church's ministry, and its hope for the future. The church, the gathering of believers who confess Christ as Lord, has continued to be an embodiment of community and common ground over history. For this reason, the church is called to model community and must help the world achieve common ground, while believing that unity

among human beings is possible – and community is fully evident - only if there is real justice for all people.

The development of common ground for the common good thus requires God-connectedness through the inspiration of the Holy Spirit. Like Christ, as has been previously intimated, it has been suggested that Howard Thurman was a "God-intoxicated man," and as such offered a paradigm of God-centered and God-inspired ministry. Perhaps, it is the case today that Christians today are beckoned to live likewise in a "God-intoxicated" way, as we seek to bring about the common ground and the common good among us.

At the root of American Protestantism has been an ongoing quest for an appropriation of common ground for the common good. Martin Luther's call for the reformation of the church in the 16th century seemed to signal a call for Christian communities to address matters of ecclesial, theological and socio-political significance to the masses of people. By its very nature, Reformation faith and Protestantism served as a faithful protest against what was perceived – at least to some degree – as the class abuses of the church and society – directed primarily at the disinherited (the poor). In as much as the Protestant Reformation was to become a protest against some of the practices of the church - as perceived by Luther and others - it would also become a framework for reforming and reframing some of the practices of Christianity in the search for common ground and the common good.

The quest for such common ground became one of the marks of enlightenment faith that would be the hallmark of early Protestantism in America. Martin Marty intimates in his book *Pilgrims in their Own Land* that although early 15th and 16th century settlers in the American colonies were largely "pilgrims of dissent," what they shared was a common quest for freedom, and that colonists were "knit together by law, religion, and custom."[242]

Much of the quest for an appropriation of the common ground and common good in the late 19th and early 20th centuries can be viewed against the philosophical and ethical backdrop of utilitarianism. Although there continues to be a great deal of debate as to the merits of utilitarianism as a philosophical and ethical construct, at least in some measure, it was the thinking of Jeremy Bentham and John Stuart Mill, among others, and their notion of "utility" that provided a framework to talk about what is good, and thus what brings about the common good. Thus, a critical question of utilitarianism is, "What is it that brings about the "the greatest possible good for the greatest possible number of individuals?"

In the social teachings of virtually every American Protestant denomination, there has been (and continues to be) an expressed concern for the common good. For instance, in foundational documents of the Presbyterian, Episcopal and Lutheran churches, among other mainline Protestant denominations, there are statements which point to concerns for the common good within the denominations themselves, within the context of the churches' ecumenical and interfaith relations, and within the context of the broader society.

In the Methodist churches/denominations – which I am most familiar - the theology and practice of communality, common ground and common good finds a primary point of reference at the place of John Wesley's notion of social holiness – where the concern for vital piety and communal religious practice (worship) is coupled with concerns for acts of mercy and justice – as seen in social witness, societal engagement and concern for the common good. Thus, a primary theological mandate of churches/denominations in the Wesleyan tradition(s) was and has continued to be "to reform the nation and spread scriptural holiness."

In much of the social teaching of the black churches as an institution, there is imbedded the ideological insistence on common ground as a theological, sociological and ethical frame of reference. In his book, *The Social Teaching of the Black Churches,* Peter Paris posited that two primary instruments of social reform and communal power employed by black churches were (1) the biblical idea of the parenthood of God and the kinship of all people, and (2) the constitutional idea that all people are created equally and endowed by their Creator with certain inalienable rights. Paris asserted that neither violence nor colonization ever gained domicile in the black churches, even though a few people from time to time have pushed for such strategies. In their struggle against racism, black churches have never understood themselves as a narrow self-interest group seeking their own satisfaction.[243]

In American Christianity, and certainly in the Protestantism of the early and mid-20th century, there continued to be a clear quest for an appropriation of the common good. This is perhaps most clearly seen in an articulation of the Social Gospel by Walter Rauschenbusch. In his seminal work, *A Theology of the Social Gospel*, Rauschenbusch states that "we have a social gospel." [244]

For Rauschenbusch, the Gospel of Christ, by its very nature is "social" and has communal implications. Rauschenbusch's ministry and work in New York City laid the foundation for a clear movement in many Protestant circles in the mid-20th century towards the predominant appropriation of evangelical liberalism – as also espoused by the likes of Howard Thurman. Like Rauschenbusch, Thurman would assert that the Gospel by its very nature is "social" and concerned with the common ground and the common good.

According to Rauschenbusch, "the Kingdom of God is not simply a matter of getting people to heaven, but of transforming the life on earth into the harmony of heaven."[245] Adherents of the Social Gospel Movement promoted a progressive form of Christianity, which sought to address concrete spiritual and material needs of people.

The Social Gospel, as expressed by Rauschenbusch and others, involves several tenets, including -

1. God is on the side of the oppressed. The most vulnerable are to be given preference.

2. Salvation is a material concern, as much as it is a spiritual concern. The Gospel beckons believers to work for improved housing, education, healthcare and other benefits for the less fortunate.

3. Salvation is a communal as much as an individual concern. To honor God, people must put aside their own earthly desires and help other people, especially the needy.

4. It is rooted in social-ethical teachings of Christ (Luke 4:18-19; Matthew 5). The way of Christ is to emulate the life of Jesus Christ.

5. There is an interest in the systematic redistribution of power and resources (social, economic, political). There also is a concern for the redistribution of wealth. In the Social Gospel, the purpose of wealth is not to accumulate and hoard it, but to share it with other, less fortunate people.

6. The prophetic voice is equally important as the priestly, and Christians (ministers and laity) should be engaged in the public square.

7. The church is not a servant of the state, but a critic of the state. This was clearly intimated by Martin Luther King Jr, another adherent of a form of the Social Gospel. King stated that "the church must be reminded that it is not the master or servant of the state, but rather the conscience of the state. It must be the guide and critic of the state, and never its tool."[246]

Love, Freedom and Common Ground

Love and freedom permit the individual to live the committed life that works for community. "Commitment" is also a major theme of Thurman's theology. In his book, *Disciplines of the Spirit,* it is the first discipline considered. Without commitment, the other disciplines, in Thurman's construct of community-building (growth, suffering, prayer and love), are meaningless. Commitment orders, focuses, defines and channels the use of one's resources. It also moves the individual from a false self-centeredness. It illumines the reality that "our life is not our own" – that life is lived in interdependence with our fellow men and women, interdependence with nature, and most important of all, interdependence with God. This awareness not only devotes life to an other-than-self concern, but in devotion, the self is given a greater sense of its own meaning.[247]

Human freedom, then, is essential to love's commitment towards community-building. Thurman felt that such freedom is not only essential, but is always operative. A person never loses the opportunity, and therefore the responsibility, for creating community. A person keeps the initiative over the living of his or her life.

As was previously shared, Thurman's constant quest for common ground is closely aligned with Martin Luther King,

Jr.'s later appropriation of the *Beloved Community*. Interestingly, in one of his chapters in *On God's Side*, Jim Wall posits that "The Beloved Community Welcomes All Tribes."[248] Wallis shares a quote from King that "our goal is to create a beloved community and this will require a qualitative change in our souls as well as a quantitative change in our lives." This sentiment also captures Thurman's vision of common ground and radically inclusive community.

The *Beloved Community* – the loving community of peace, justice and equality - can only be attained by loving means. Community cannot be built on the tools of hatred. Nonviolence responds in a caring way to the perpetrator of violence. It announces that the well-being of the individuals involved is of ultimate concern. It moves the level of confrontation to a higher spiritual plane. Instead of merely defeating one's offender physically or psychologically, one begins to create the climate for love to be a force, which has to be dealt with within the context of relationships and fellowship. The presence of loving care and concern introduces new possibilities for reconciliation and community. Only nonviolence permits love to enter conflict creatively and address the prevailing spiritual ills of separation, fear and hatred.

Concluding Thoughts: Thurman and the Quest for Common Ground

Thurman's lifetime quest was to bring coherency to the nature of the inner spiritual life within the context of racism and disunity in the church and society, and then help persons move to a more pronounced sense of common ground and radically inclusive community. He intimated that "There are two questions that we have to ask ourselves. The first is "Where am

I going?", and the second "Who will go with me?" If you ever get these questions in the wrong order, you are in trouble." This, in essence speaks to his understanding of the search for common ground among us.

Along these same lines, community cannot for long feed on itself; it can only flourish with the coming of others from beyond, their unknown and undiscovered sisters and brothers. For Thurman, community is essential to life, and it is this belief that moved and motivated him. It is out of this deep sense of burden and passion for community that he was able to see how detrimental and destructive racism and other forms of social disintegration are to community because they deny, denigrate and destroy people based on external and surface qualities.

Thurman insisted that the search for common ground is a universal search among all of humanity. He stated that "A person is always threatened in one's very ground by a sense of isolation, by feeling oneself cut off from one's fellows. Yet, the person can never separate oneself from one's fellows, for mutual interdependence is characteristic of all life."[249] Thus, as has been shared, for him, this universal quest and search for common ground has teleological implications as it essentially provides the framework for the meaning of life itself.

CHAPTER SEVEN
ACROSS DIVIDES –
TOWARDS A GOSPEL OF RADICAL INCLUSIVITY FOR
THE 21ST CENTURY CHURCH AND SOCIETY

"It cannot be denied that too often the weight of the Christian movement has been on the side of the strong and the powerful and against the weak and oppressed - this, despite the gospel."
– Howard Thurman

Dimensions and Dynamics of Diversity in the 21st Century

The world today is fraught with social, economic, political and religious upheaval. Over the past several years, in the United States and across the globe, we have become more divided along various lines. In the U.S., the social and political division that we now experience is not really new, but it challenges our sense of normalcy in ways that perhaps we have not been challenged in the past.

This division exists against the backdrop of a burgeoning diversity in the U.S. and in other parts of the world. I had the opportunity to address a group of more than 200 scholars in South Bend, Indiana in 2015 where those in attendance were mostly North American, but interestingly the group included persons who were nearly equally Muslim, Jewish and Christian – and nearly equally white, black, Hispanic and Asian. I sense that this type of interreligious, intercultural engagement was not unique to that setting, but in some circles is being challenged and brought into question in light of the overarching concern of what it means to be "American" today.

A part of America's sense of who it says it is etched in one of our national credos – the Latin phrase *e pluribus unum* –

"Out of Many One." The implication here is that the U.S, has been, and continues to be, a nation of many. It is a nation of many cultures and ethnicities, many classes and social locations, many religions and geographies, female and male, with many persuasions and ways of identifying what it means to be human. And yet, the vision that the nation says it shares within the context of this "many" is a vision of somehow also becoming "one".

In any event, there exists the challenge of living into this grand vision of *e pluribus unum*. Perhaps it is "Divides", then, which most clearly characterize the U.S. today, both in society and within religious communities. These "Divides" are seen in that we are Brown, White, Black, Asian and Indigenous, LGBTQIA+ and 'straight", poor, working class, middle class and wealthy, Republican, Democrat and Independent, south and north, west and east, rural, suburban and urban, conservative, moderate and liberal, evangelical and progressive, non-denominational and mainline. These "Divides" are seen in that – politically and religiously – the U.S. today is red, blue and indeed purple (yes purple).

Washington, DC – Anacostia and the Tale of Two Cities

I was born in Washington, DC in the 1960's. It was at a time when – although I did not realize it until I was a teenager – the Nation's Capital was effectively a segregated the city. I grew up in a section of DC called Anacostia. For persons who have grown up in the District of Columbia, lived there for any period of time, or visited and stayed for any length of time, we have come to realize that "Anacostia" in many ways is a euphemism for what it means to live east of the Anacostia River. This river effectively divides DC into east and west, and divides the city in more general ways along lines of what it means to grow up relatively poorer or richer – which is generally evident in the quality of schools, hospitals, policing/safety, roads, food/nutrition, stores, housing, and so on. In many ways, to borrow a theme from Charles Dickens' great novel, this speaks to *the tale of two cities*.

Over time, I came to realize that to have been reared in Anacostia carried with it a number of assumptions about who one might become, and the length and breadth of one's likely social mobility in life. To be from Anacostia effectively meant that one was reared in a socially and physically segregated space which at the time of my upbringing was well over 85 percent Black, and largely populated by poor, working-class, and at-best barely above middle-class persons.

This is to say that growing up, to go anywhere west of the Anacostia River meant to cross over into another completely different socio-economic reality. This pronounced "Divide" in the nation's capital did not really dawn on me until I enrolled in Wesley Theological Seminary to begin my theological studies in my mid-20's. Wesley Seminary is located on the far northwest end of the city in one of the wealthiest neighborhoods in the nation (Ward 3), and taking the drive for three years to seminary from my home, which was by then in a suburban neighborhood not far from where I had grown up in Anacostia, I would drive across this physical and social "Divide" daily. I'd drive across the Anacostia River through drug-infested, "blue light" neighborhoods where many young men and women would feel blessed to live to young adulthood. Then I'd drive past the national Capitol building, and the grand embassies which house international diplomats; I would drive by exclusive private clubs, which growing up, I did not even realize existed, and finally I'd arrive each day at Wesley Seminary.

A Theoretical Framework for Discussing "Divide" and "Inclusivity"

An overarching concern in addressing the matter of societal and ecclesial "Divides" regards what it means for faith communities to be relevant today. The reality is that America and the world are rapidly changing. No longer can we simply view ourselves in terms of black and white, Protestant and Catholic. Lewis Brown Griggs and Lente-Louise Louw, editors of the series of works *"Valuing Diversity: New Tools for a New Reality"*, have suggested that differences in culture, ethnicity, gender, race, perspectives, personality, style, values and feelings need to be honored and encouraged, not merely tolerated. [250] The real value of diversity is that it produces synergistic interactions across "Divides". It is this synergy that produces unpredictable consequences in terms of breakthrough and results.

To place the yearning for human interaction and connectedness into context, the African construct of *Ubuntu* is most helpful. *Ubuntu* is a Zulu term that speaks to the quality of being human that is imbedded in all of humanity by virtue of the fact that we are all human. *Ubuntu* thus binds us together as a human family. It essentially states that, "I am because you are, and because you are, therefore, I am". It manifests itself through various human acts, clearly visible in social, political and economic situations, as well as among family and forms of community.

A commitment to the realization of *Ubuntu* offers hope for the world in which we live. Jims Wallis points to the *Ubuntu* theology of Archbishop Desmond Tutu as practiced during the fight against Apartheid in South Africa as being a sign of hope for a movement towards appropriating (and re-appropriating) radically inclusive community in the 21st century.[251] A quote from Tutu emphasizes the criticality of *Ubuntu*, "You might have much of the world's riches, and might have a portion of authority, but if you have no *Ubuntu*, you do not amount to much."

According to sociolinguist Buntu Mfentana, *Ubuntu* "runs through the veins of Africans." Louw elaborates and states that the quality of being human for Africans is embodied in the oft-repeated proverb, "A person is a person through other people."[252]

Ubuntu essentially speaks to the yearning towards radically inclusive community. Community – common ground – by its very nature - is integrative; it speaks to a "common unity" among us. Radically inclusive community includes persons of different races, genders, ages, religions, cultures, viewpoints, lifestyles, and stages of development - and serves to integrate persons into a whole that is greater – more actualized and dynamic – than the sum of its parts. Forms of disintegration and disunity are, therefore, to be understood as being antithetical to the common good, community and to the will of God.

What's at stake the light of the practice of theology in the 21st Century West?

Research data shows that the United States continues to become more diverse or "different". This diversity is seen in that, according to U.S. Census Bureau and Pew Research Center data –

- Whites are the slowest growing segment of the U.S. population at .5%. Projections indicate that there will be a White minority (or no racial/ethnic majority) in the U.S. by 2044.

- There are at least 3.3 million Muslims in the U.S., and that number is likely to double by 2050.
- There are at least 55.3 million Hispanics in the U.S. (17.4% of the population), with a projected 120 million Hispanics in the U.S. by 2060.
- Asians make up 5.8% of the U.S. population, and make up 36% of immigrants, overtaking Hispanics. China is the fastest growing immigrant group in the U.S., passing Mexico.
- The 2nd fastest growing racial group in the U.S. is those claiming 2 or more races (bi-racial and multi-racial persons). This group has grown to at least 6.6 million people; 3.1% of the population.
- 41% of the world's migrants live in the West (*Christianity Today*).

(sources: U.S. Census Bureau (2010), Pew Research Data, *Christianity Today*)

The Church and the Racial Divide

As it regards the church and the problem of race in America today (as one form of "Divide"), in many ways, a pall remains over much – if not most - of the contemporary church. *Racism continues to be the elephant in America's living room.* In reflecting on the state of the church in his day, Howard Thurman stated:

It is in order now at last to raise the question: Is the witness of the church in our society the unfolding of such an idea as we see manifested in the religious experience and the life of Jesus? Whatever may be the delimiting character of the historical development of the church, the simple fact remains that at the present moment in our society, as an institution, the church is divisive and discriminating, even within its fellowship. It is divided into dozens of splinters. This would indicate that it is essentially sectarian in character. As an institution there is no such thing as the church. There has to be some kind of church..."[253]

Thurman further stated:

To those who need profound succor and strength to enable them to live in the present with dignity and creativity, Christianity often has been sterile and of little avail. The conventional Christian word is muffled, confused and vague. Too often the price exacted by society for security and respectability is that the Christian movement in its formal expression must be on the side of the strong against the weak. This is a matter of tremendous significance, for it reveals to what extent a religion that was born of people acquainted with persecution and suffering has become the cornerstone of a civilization and of nations whose very position in modern life has too often been secured by ruthless use of power applied to weak and defenseless people.[254]

In their book, *Divided by Faith: Evangelical Religion and the Problem of Race,* Michael Emerson and Christian Smith developed a theory to explain why churches are racially exclusive enclaves despite Christianity's ideals about being inclusive. According to Emerson and Smith, Americans choose where and with whom to worship; race is one of the most important grounds on which they choose; so the more choices they have, the more their religious institutions will be segregated.[255]

Through sociological analysis, Emerson and Smith tested their theory and found it to be valid. Churches are more segregated than schools, workplaces or neighborhoods. The least segregated sector of American society is also the least governed by choice; it's the military. Because white Protestants are the largest religious community in the U.S., they have the greatest choice as to with whom to gather. The authors point out that ninety-five percent of churches are effectively racially segregated, with 80 percent or more of their members being of the same race.[256]

The result is that about 5 percent of religious congregations in the U.S. can fairly be considered multicultural/multiracial, with the majority of Christians engaging in what sociologists call homophily, or the desire to congregate with "birds of the same feather," with their congregations reflecting ethnoracial particularism.[257]

"Table" as a Model of Meeting for Developing Radically Inclusive Community

Since 2006, I have had the privilege of leading groups of scholars from Wesley Theological Seminary and St. Mary's Seminary and University in immersion courses that retrace many of the steps of the American Civil Rights movement in Alabama during the 1950's and 60's. These groups are typically comprised of 7-30 masters or doctoral level students, faculty and staff, and we travel for up to two weeks through Birmingham, Montgomery and Selma, Alabama.

On all of these immersion experiences, the groups of participants have been very socially diverse. We are women and men, Native Americans, Hispanics, Whites, Asians and Blacks. We are from various Christian denominations.

We begin each day with singing, praying and reading Scripture as was the practice in the tradition of the American Civil Rights movement. John Lewis, now a U.S. Congressman from Georgia, and one who labored on the front lines of the Civil Rights movement, has intimated that "We never went out without singing and praying." And so before leaving each morning, we pray, read Scripture, and sing freedom songs like "Oh Freedom," "We Shall Overcome," "There is a Balm", and "Ain't Gon' Let Nobody Turn Me Around."

As we travel, reflect, listen and learn together - struggling through many of the difficult paths and realities of those who lived the Civil Rights movement - we invariably sense among ourselves the real possibility that radically inclusive community – the *Beloved Community* - can be realized in our lifetime, and that bridges can indeed be built to help us cross and healthily engage those things that still divide us.

We visit and study at numerous sites that were significant to the Civil Rights movement. In Montgomery, we visit Dexter Avenue King Memorial Baptist Church, where Rev. Dr. Martin Luther King, Jr. served as pastor from 1954-1960 at the height of the Montgomery Bus Boycott and other significant Civil Rights events. Just two blocks from Dexter Avenue Church, we visit the First Confederate White House - the home of Jefferson Davis, the president of the Confederacy. Sitting between Dexter Avenue Church and the first Confederate White House is the Alabama State Capitol – the place where Governor George Wallace and other state officials stood in defiance of any efforts towards integration and equal rights among the races, and where Wallace notoriously exclaimed, *"Segregation now, segregation tomorrow, segregation forever.* " We visit the Equal Justice Initiative, and learn of the legacy of lynching across America, as well as instances of modern injustice like mass incarceration.

In Birmingham, one of the places we visit is the Sixteenth Street Baptist Church, which on September 15, 1963 was bombed by segregationists, and where four black girls (ages 11-14) were killed in the church basement while preparing for their Children's Day worship celebration. Across the street from the Sixteenth Street Baptist Church is Kelly Ingram Park, where many of the protest marches in the city of Birmingham began, and which became notorious for the atrocious and brutal acts of Police Commissioner Eugene "Bull" Connor and the Birmingham police as they turned dogs and fire hoses on black children of Birmingham.

In Selma, we walk across the Edmund Pettus Bridge, which was the site of "Bloody Sunday" on March 7, 1965 - when hundreds of blacks and some whites gathered in an effort to march across the bridge towards Montgomery to demand voting rights, only to be violently tear-gassed, cattle-prodded, bloodily beaten and turned back by state and local authorities. In Selma, we also visit Brown Chapel African Methodist Episcopal Church, the place where over 600 persons gathered to sing, pray, strategize and receive marching orders in their ongoing efforts to take the 54 mile journey from Selma to Montgomery.

Each time we journey, my memory harkens back to one of our earlier trips, where Eileen Guenther, a professor at Wesley Seminary who was a part of that study group, offered that it was a spiritual sung by many choirs, "I'm Gonna Sit at the Welcome Table," that played in her head throughout our experience.[258] These tables are –

- *Lunch counters of restaurants where all had not been welcome (in the past);*

- *The dining room table in the parsonage of Dexter Avenue Baptist Church, in Montgomery, where we were told, the Southern Christian Leadership Conference was formed;*

- *The kitchen table of the same parsonage where Dr. King searched his soul and felt God telling him to press on with his work;*

- *The tables at which the people at 16th Street Baptist Church served us lunch, tables placed adjacent to the site of the tragic bombing in September 1963 that killed four young girls;*

- *The tables around which members of our group gathered to share stories as victims of discrimination, of their courageous work in the Civil Rights movement (and other freedom and human rights movements), and their lament over a lack of awareness of what was going on at that time in America's history.*

- *Tables around which we laughed and cried together – celebrating how far we've come, yet realizing the pain inflicted upon those who made it possible for us to be able to sit at table together in light of those things that could yet still be in place to divide us.*

At the conclusion of each of these Alabama intercultural immersions, I am invariably struck by how far we as a society have come, how many "Divides" we've crossed, and yet how many "Divides" are yet to be crossed. There is a real sense of hope – and a real sense of the presence of God in our small, diverse groups - as together we choose to become radically inclusive community. We realize that it would not have been possible 50 years ago for 7-30 people from diverse backgrounds to travel and study in relative peace and safety throughout Alabama. For me, these are real signs of the stones of hope that can, as Martin Luther King, Jr. spoke about on August 28, 1963 on the steps of the Lincoln Memorial in Washington, DC, be hewn out of the mountain of despair among us. These are real signs of the footprints of the dream that Howard Thurman wrote of in reflecting on the experience of the Church for the Fellowship of All Peoples (1944-53), real signs that radically inclusive community can emerge.

A Seminary Panel and Hope for the Future

A panel conversation of seminary students that I was a part of in 2015 gives further evidence of the possibilities of how radically inclusive community can emerge. This experience sheds light on matters that might be given attention in thinking on the future of the church and society.

My first observation about this seminary panel was the diversity of the group. Five of the six panelists were in their 20's or early 30's. They had arrived at seminary from six different places – Chicago, New York City, the Dominican Republic, Zimbabwe, Mississippi and Virginia. None had come from the city where they were now attending seminary. They were United Methodist (4), African Methodist Episcopal (1), and Baptist (1). They were Korean, Latino, African, White and African-American. Four were women.

This diversity reflects that of this particular seminary, and points to the fact that society today looks quite different than it did forty years ago, and that perhaps this type of broadening diversity is reflective of where the church of today may need to move.

As these six students reflected on their seminary experiences and how they thought their theological education would impact their future role as religious leaders, it was clear that each of them had a vision of the church and their role in religious leadership that would move the church beyond traditional notions of what the church has been, and is to be, institutionally. And thus, theirs were visions that shifted conceptions of Christian ministry and the ways in which church leadership might be practiced in the future.

The collective insights/observations of these seminarians pointed to prospects of the 21st century church living into new and exciting forms of inclusivity, and prospects of churches of the future being shaped in ways that give impetus to several foundational concerns. Succinctly stated, these concerns are that:

1. The church must be led towards deeper, more intentional exploration and growth in the practice of *spiritual disciplines* as means of deepening personal faith and creating community.

2. The church must engage in processes that encourage the ongoing development of competencies in the *art of leadership* that are sensitive to cultural inclusivity and the changes that are incumbent in post-modern, post-Christian reality.

3. The church must facilitate reflection/action relative to the burgeoning *globality* in our midst.

4. The church must facilitate an ongoing understanding and deeper engagement with *youth and young adult cultures (Millennials and Post-millennials)*, which typically understand and appropriate the merging of cultures on

levels that are more profound and pronounced than it has been for previous generations.

5. The church must facilitate constructive engagement, theological discourse and intersectional analysis across *cultures and theological/faith perspectives*.

6. The church must have the capacity to continue in organizing, developing and cultivating *strong partnerships and collaborations* (with students, local churches, judicatories, interfaith, non-profit and non-religious entities).

In summary, a hope is that wherever and whenever necessary, we in the churches and society begin to clearly see the "Divides", interconnections and intersections that exist within the contexts of racism, sexism, classism, militarism and heterosexism. These can be seen as the quintuplets of evil today. Oppression is oppression in whatever forms it presents itself, and devising means of engaging and addressing it will be critical to the church and society in the future. The development of competencies and capacity in these and other areas within the 21st century churches will serve to help in building bridges and crossing the many "Divides" and, moving toward radically inclusive community in the years to come.

CHAPTER EIGHT
COME GO WITH ME -
A GOSPEL OF RADICAL INCLUSIVITY

"Keep alive the dream; for as long as a man has a dream in his heart, he cannot lose the significance of living." – Howard Thurman

In the final analysis, Howard Thurman's theological project was rooted in concerns for the disinherited and a quest of radical inclusivity in the church and society. These concerns were intricately connected to his yearning for an irreducible essence as rooted in a search for a Christ-centered spirituality and sense of connectedness with God. Thurman's Christology - and the explication of the identity of Jesus of Nazareth in his work - was foundational to his overall theological project.

He spoke to the need for overcoming exclusion, racial hatred and social disintegration, and advanced the appropriation of the Christian love-ethic as foundational for constructively moving toward radically inclusive community. For him, the ability and willingness to overcome hatred and fear derived out of his conception of the love of God. God's love is redemptive in that God loves humanity so much that God demonstrated love for the world by offering God's son, Christ, to the world.

Thurman himself sought to be an instrument of peace, reconciliation and radical inclusivity. The prayer of St. Francis of Assisi speaks to Thurman's commitment and vision for radically inclusive community:

> Lord, make me an instrument of your peace,
> Where there is hatred, let me sow love,
> Where there is injury, pardon,

Where there is doubt, faith,
Where there is despair, hope,
Where there is darkness, light,
Where there is sadness, joy.[259]

The striving towards radically inclusive community has been one of the most consistent strivings among humans over the course of history. Radically inclusive community is to be understood as God's ideal way of life, the way of Christ, for a heretofore broken and disintegrated humanity. The apostle Paul's words to the church at Ephesus speak to the contemporary challenge of the church and society, and the common and persistent hope for community that is found in Christ:

> "Christ Jesus is our peace; in his flesh he has made all groups into one and has broken down the dividing wall, that is, the hostility between us… and reconciles groups to God in one body through the cross. So then you are no longer strangers and aliens, but you are citizens with the saints and also members of the household of God, built upon the foundation of the apostles and prophets, with Christ Jesus himself as the cornerstone. In him the whole structure is joined together and grows into a holy temple in the Lord; in whom you also are built together spiritually into a dwelling place for God." (Ephesians 2:14-22)

Although Thurman recognized the necessity of the just and equitable distribution of power in social relationships, his primary concern was with the individual's response to unjust political and economic arrangements, which is equally important in the quest for social justice.[260] Thurman was aware that the existence of injustice anywhere is a threat to justice everywhere. Likewise, the pervasiveness of non-community and social disintegration threatened the actualization of true community among all persons. It is then not only appropriate, but necessary for each person in society to be actively concerned about the injustice that affects other persons, and to then work diligently and constructively to promote radically inclusive community.

Eight summary observations can be drawn from Thurman's life and work as have been previously discussed throughout this volume:

1. For Thurman, epistemologically and praxiologically, ministry and theology are to be understood as acts of both "head and heart", mind and spirit (both/and). Thus, Thurman has been variously viewed as a mystic-prophet and pastor-theologian.

2. Thurman's work (pastoring, teaching and writing) speaks to the perennial concerns of persons across denominations, faith perspectives and other forms of difference as to how to live from a spiritual center, and how to integrate matters of the "head and heart."

3. His search for radically inclusive community is intricately connected to the yearning for an irreducible essence as rooted in his own search for a Christ-centered spirituality and sense of God-connectedness.

4. Thurman's conception of Christian love (a Christian love-ethic based on the teachings of Jesus and the

Sermon on the Mount) was rooted in the example of the unconditional love of God in Christ. The practice of unconditional love *(agape)* is essential to breaking down social barriers such as racism, classism and sexism (and other forms of social disintegration).

5. Thurman resonated with the thoughts of the likes of Josiah Royce, and later Martin Luther King, Jr., who argued that humanity, by nature, is not perfected (saved) in solitude. Only in the *Beloved Community* can we find ourselves (individually and communally), to stop being individuals and to start being the totality of who we are as God's people. This is to be understood as a theological imperative.

6. Theologically, radically inclusive community is that which brings together the totality of all persons, both individually and collectively, and provides for them a genuine identity in a disingenuous world. Humanity requires some venue through which it can experience and develop the integrated self and community.

7. For Thurman, there was no possibility of radically inclusive community (the *Beloved Community*) without careful and constructive attention to the disinherited. He proclaimed that the mistreatment of America's disinherited and acceptance of "the will to segregate" are betrayals of American and Christian ideals of community-building.

8. Reconciliation, as a spiritual discipline, as expressed in the actualization of radically inclusive community,

occurs through intentional acts of seeking to build community across forms of difference.

As this study has focused on Howard Thurman's arrival at a theology and praxis of radically inclusive community, there are several implications and principles that emerge as we have moved into the 21st century. The eight principles that follow – *acknowledgement, affirmation, authenticity, association, articulation, aspiration, anticipation and appropriation* - can be seen as a framework (template) for bringing synthesis to the thinking and praxis of Thurman, while also serving as the foundation of a contemporary model and praxis for the church and society for developing and realizing radically inclusive community in the 21st century.

1. Acknowledgement

To start, there needs to be an acknowledgement that racism, and other forms of social disintegration in America are real, and have harmed many people, and continue to do so. *Acknowledgement* essentially involves the movement from cultural/ethnocentrism to cultural/ethnorelativism. Eric Law speaks to the theological predicament of ethnocentrism when he states:

> In our towers of ethnocentrism, we put God within our cultural frame. We may be unable to distinguish the difference between our culture and God's culture. We believe that God is on our side and therefore, we can judge those who are not like us as the enemies.[261]

Cultural/ethnocentrism ultimately limits our perception of God. Jesus' challenge for us to love our enemies is an

140

invitation to enter into a new paradigm of cultural/ethnorelativism. For God does not favor one culture over another. Cultural/ethnorelativism leads to an acknowledgement and valuation of cultural differences as neither good or bad, but only different. Milton J. Bennett, identified three theoretical stages of ethnorelativity: *Acceptance, Adaptation*, and *Integration*.[262] These stages are arranged progressively according to the intercultural sensitivity developmental process, and are helpful in the movement beyond narrow conceptions of cultural identity, and towards broader perspectives of what and whom God may be inviting persons to become as community.

Howard Thurman spoke to the divine and moral imperative – the calling - that Christians share in seeking to eradicate racial hatred and social disintegration, and advanced the appropriation of the Christian love-ethic as foundational for constructively moving toward the realization of radically inclusive community. He asserted that God's intent is for the human family to live in community as interrelated members. Jesus came into the world to call persons back into community.

Consequently, there is the obligation to treat every person as Christ Himself, respecting his/her life as if it were the life of Christ. Even if the other person proves to be unjust, wicked and odious to us, we cannot take upon ourselves a final and definitive judgment in their case. We still have an obligation to be patient, and to seek their highest spiritual interests. In other words, we are formally commanded to love our enemies, and this obligation cannot be met by a formula of words.[263]

In *acknowledgement,* there must also be recognition of God's divine imperative that radically inclusive community be effected, and then there must be an expressed intent to act on such recognition. In *Disciplines of the Spirit*, Thurman highlighted not only the search for unity in a broken human community, but also the desire to remedy the lack of harmony within the individual. All this seeks out a state of wholeness which is the natural state of life as intended in the creation.[264] He affirmed this concept in this excerpt from his work, *The Search For Common Ground*, "the (person) who seeks community with his own spirit, who searches for it in his experiences with the literal facts of the external world, who makes this his formal intent as he seeks to bring order out of the chaos of his collective life, is not going against life but will be sustained and supported by life."[265]

Raleigh Washington and Glen Kehrein in *Breaking Down Walls: A Model for Reconciliation in the Age of Racial Strife,* refer to the concept of God's imperative as "*call*."[266] Acknowledging the divine imperative for persons to move toward radically inclusive community essentially involves the process of answering the questions, "What does God call me to be as a part of community? What does God call the church and society to become as community?" An acknowledgement of divine calling has the purpose of leading us into critical and constructive reflection and action that is beyond our human initiative, proclivities, inclinations, desires, abilities and comfort zones.

2. *Affirmation*

As has been noted, as an African American, Howard Thurman possessed a perspective on Christian faith that had been forged on the anvil of slavery, segregation and violent forms of racial oppression. In light of this, he consistently affirmed that all humanity was bound together through our common creator. Hence for Thurman, the fundamental tenets of love, prayer, forgiveness and reconciliation were to be the spiritual means of addressing extant forms of oppression and social disintegration. In a world that is still plagued with brokenness, separation, suspicion and deadly conflicts along racial, tribal, and ethnic lines, it remains the urgent calling of Christians to affirm that God created all persons, and that we are called to exist in peaceable, just and radically inclusive community.

The recognition and valuation of diversity entails affirming several presumptions about God the creator, and the humanity that has been created by God. Christian ethicist J. Phillip Wogaman refers to this as the method of positive presumption.[267] According to Wogaman, we presume: (1) *The goodness of created existence.* God created humanity (all humans) in goodness and wholeness. God's divine intention for created humanity is goodness and wholeness (shalom). (2) *The value of human life.* In each human being there is sacred and infinite worth as a result of humanity's creation in God's image (imago dei). (3) *The unity of the human family.* Humans have not been created to live in a vacuum, but in community with one another. Because of our creation by the same God, we are all interconnected and interrelated. (4) *The equality of all persons in God.* As God created all persons in the image of God, and as there is unity among humans in God, there is also equality among all human beings.

Henry Mitchell and Nicholas Cooper-Lewter pointed out in *Soul Theology* that equality is not merely political rhetoric; it involves God's justice expressed impartially.[268] With regard to equality, they further stated:

Either God regards all persons as intrinsically equal, or (God) is the unjust author of inequity, the very Creator of the oppressions suffered by persons and groups at the bottom of the social and economic system. As easy as it may be to practice inequality, the American dream will not permit it to be approved by the Creator...The founders of this nation attributed their egalitarian dogma to the very mind of God, and so Americans have believed ever since.

This equality is not to be mistaken for uniformity, however. Americans come in different sizes and shapes. They have various levels of giftedness, in a further diversified spectrum of specialties. They represent a fantastic variety of colors and cultures, from every corner of the earth, to say nothing of the profusion of personality patterns. Still, before the law, they are all equal in standing. Few affirmations have more sweeping consequences psychologically and spiritually, as well as legally, and few are so inadequately articulated, especially in America's circle of power. The pluralism of the dream is far better understood today than ever, but the drift toward the tyranny of single-group supremacy and enforced uniformity is always present.[269]

The familiar Negro spiritual speaks to the notion of the equality that intrinsically exists among persons:
The fare is cheap, and all can ride,
the rich and the poor are there.
No second class aboard this train,
no difference in the fare.
Oh, get on board, little children,
get on board, little children,

Get on board, little children,
there room for many a'more.[270]

Christ's love for all humanity was redemptive in that despite human faults and frailties, he willingly gave his life for us. "God demonstrated love toward us, in that while we were yet sinners, Christ died for (humanity)" (Romans 5:8). Thus, hatred and fear are overcome in the various forms that they manifest themselves in human relationships through God's redemptive love in Christ, who "is our peace."

Christ came into the world as the Prince of Peace. Thomas Merton asserts that we know that Christ himself is our peace. We believe that God has chosen Godself in the Mystical Body of Christ, an elect people, regenerated by the Blood of the Savior, and committed by their baptismal promise to wage war upon the evil and hatred that are in man, and help to establish the Kingdom of God and of peace.[271] This means a recognition that human nature, identical in all (persons), was assumed by the Logos in the Incarnation, and that Christ died out of love for all (persons), in order to live in all (human beings).[272]

It is clear throughout Scripture that Christians are called to lives that are characterized by radical inclusivity. Christianity and community are virtually synonymous. An essential mark of the church is *koinonia* – fellowship, community. The church is called to model radically inclusive community for the broader world. In the commonality among persons, there is unity in Christ. The biblical record makes it clear that Christ intended for the church to be a unified body. Some of the Lord's final words in a prayer were "That they may be one" (John 17:21).

In light of God's ideal of individual and communal wholeness (*shalom*) the church is called to be the Body of

Christ (1 Corinthians 12:27). Each member of the Body is connected to the others, as branches are connected to their root, or vine. As Christ's body, we are connected to each other in, for, and because of Christ, the "true vine" (John 15:1). The Body of Christ is then understood as an organic and living entity, dependent upon its vine as the source of its being – its energy and life. And as the body is dependent upon the vine for its existence, it also depends upon each of its members, or branches, which comprise community.

Amidst human diversity, there must be a comprehension and affirmation of the intrinsic equality of all persons. The apostle Paul stated, "There is neither Jew or Greek, there is neither bond or free, there is neither male or female; for you are all one in Christ Jesus" (Galatians 3:28).

As the Body of Christ, the church is to serve as an integrative bridge for the many societal entities with which it relates. One way that this might be accomplished is by striving towards racial and cultural pluralism, which reflects the diversity among peoples. A comprehension and appropriation of pluralism is an important asset in the movement toward radically inclusive community.[273] A critical issue, therefore, remains how to affirm our shared humanity and discover common ground among persons from different cultural, socioeconomic, political, racial and even religious backgrounds.

3. *Authenticity*

Howard Thurman asserted that community – by its very nature - is authentic. As was pointed out earlier in this volume, it was as co-pastor of the Church for the Fellowship of All Peoples that Thurman began to most profoundly sense the possibilities of the gospel of Jesus Christ being a means towards realizing radical inclusivity. In his words, "we were convinced that a way could be found to create a religious fellowship worthy of transcending racial, cultural and social distinctions."[274]   In Thurman's estimation, for a moment in time, that group of people was able to authentically celebrate their diversity, affirm their common humanity and achieve a state of being, which was the essence of inclusive fellowship.

Authentic interaction among persons of different cultural groups ultimately results in the need for reconciliation. Reconciliation is more than the absence of violence. It must include recognition of the equal worth of all, and must actively embrace peace with justice.   It is what Dietrich Bonhoeffer called "a costly grace."[275] The heart of the gospel warrants a profound encounter between persons and among peoples. At the center of Christian faith, Jesus reconciles persons to God. He also reconciles persons to each other. He is the One who "breaks down the dividing wall and makes us one."

As long as human beings – each with incumbent and distinctive fears, insecurities and the instinct to survive - seek to interrelate, conflict will be an inevitable aspect of the movement toward community.   For radically inclusive community to emerge, there must be the will to act intentionally – sometimes against human instinct – in order to develop the space in which people of different backgrounds can not only tolerate each other, but develop the capacity to understand and appreciate one another even though they may not always agree.

Authenticity is closely related to sincerity. In their work together in Chicago, Raleigh Washington and Glen Kehrein noted the importance of sincerity in seeking to relate across cultures. According to Washington and Kehrein, sincerity is a willingness to be vulnerable, including self-disclosure of feelings, attitudes, differences and perceptions with the goal of resolution and building trust. Additionally, they pointed out that intentionality is important in building multicultural relationships and community. Intentionality is the purposeful, positive and planned activity that facilitates reconciliation. Sincerity and intentionality are two principles that are closely related.[276]

In radically inclusive community, unconditional love must be embraced and embodied. This involves compassion and the willingness to listen to others. Compassion is the ability to empathetically enter into the suffering of another and experience it from the inside. We can have compassion even for those who do evil; for they suffer from a blindness and a darkness that prevent them from seeing truth. [277]

Authenticity is rooted in the premise that we are inevitably our brother/sister's keeper. Whatever affects one directly, affects all indirectly.[278] Thus, we are led to live in solidarity with the marginalized and disinherited among us. Gilbert Caldwell, in *Race, Racism and Reconciliation,* asserts that the church must discover ways to "be in solidarity with the poor" among us. Caldwell further posits that the church must remember to act on what it believes:

> We believe God is creator and parent. God is an equal opportunity creator and parent. We are not created by God to be rich or poor, powerful or powerless. We of the church believe that every creature on this earth was created by God, and we thus share the same parent, and we are brothers and sisters. We must see to it that our brothers and sisters do not suffer. When they suffer, we must suffer.[279]

Caldwell points to several specific ways that Christians can be authentically in solidarity with the marginalized. First, we must acknowledge that too often we represent the problem rather than the solution. Second, we must be honest about who we are, what we do, and what is important to us in terms of our lifestyle. Third, we must be consistent and persevering. Our faith does not give us the right to burn out. Fourth, we must be willing to critique systems. Fifth, we must be positive and hopeful because the gospel of the church is a gospel of hope.[280]

Marjorie Thompson in *Soul Feast: An Invitation to the Christian Spiritual Life,* speaks of *authenticity* in terms of the need for persons to practice hospitality with one another as a means of community-building:

> Our love for one another is a direct expression of our love for God. "Those who do not love their brother or sister whom they have seen, cannot love God whom they have not seen." (1 John 4:20) One of our more persistent problems is that we do not see each other as sisters or brothers, much less love each other as such.[281]

Thurman demonstrated that love, as an active, intentional means of developing radically inclusive community, carries a responsibility. When we love, we look at circumstances and people differently. We don't react negatively to the negative actions of others. When we love, we bear insults, and we tolerate mean temperaments. When we love, we exhibit kindness and gentleness though it may not be returned, we pray for those who have wronged us, we fight against injustice and strive for liberation. When we love, we show and we teach unloving people what it means to know God.

To love our neighbors as ourselves is one of the greatest commandments because it is not easily accomplished. To love our enemies is an even more daunting task. To authentically love in the face of adversity, injustice, persecution and oppression is one of the most difficult requirements of humanity. But if we can achieve it, if we can learn to love despite our circumstances, we can realize the hope for an end to violence and oppression. Thurman taught society that authentic love can conquer violence, and that when we love, we would not intentionally hurt those whom we say we love.

4. *Association*

Association involves the process of making the radical choice to be in community with those who may be different than we are. It is actively seeking to understand, and to come to value and embrace the lives of those who are the "others" among us.

Howard Thurman's life served as an example of the role of *association* in cross-cultural contexts. According to Alton Pollard, Thurman's approach to interpersonal relations is sensitive and complex: a mix of high vision, quietistic discourse, and practical intimacy.[282] Carlyle Fielding Stewart refers to the Thurman mode as "intuitive," a kind of spiritual-ethical liberation,[283] while Luther Smith notes that Thurman's "convictions are not adopted systems of belief, but convictions which have been shaped, tested, and proved within life experiences."[284] However stated, it is manifestly clear that Thurman embraced a compelling, consistent and intersubjective mode of human association in the world.

In *The Search for Common Ground*, Thurman argued that the yearning for association is a universal search among all of humanity. As earlier intimated, he stated that "A person is always threatened in one's very ground by a sense of isolation, by feeling oneself cut off from one's fellows. Yet, the person can never separate oneself from one's fellows, for mutual interdependence is characteristic of all life."[285] Thus for

Thurman, this common, universal quest association has teleological implications, as it essentially provides the framework for the meaning of life itself.

At its foundation, developing radically inclusive community involves a willingness to accept the invitation that Christ extends to us, as well as inviting others – those who may in some ways be unlike us – into dialogue and relationship. Community is the reality where persons can be themselves, and know that they have the same value as their neighbor. It is a safe reality, an inclusive reality where mutual respect and dignity prevail.

Reflection on the cultural context and diversity in which Christ sought to create radically inclusive community is insightful in seeking to arrive at a conception for association and developing radically inclusive community today. Harold Recinos, in *Jesus Weeps: Global Encounters on our Doorstep,* elaborates on the cultural environment that surrounded the town of Nazareth, and Galilee – the broader region in Palestine - during the time that Jesus lived:

> Jesus comes from a part of the world rejected by the Jerusalem establishment (Nazareth of Galilee). Within the global and culturally diverse context of Galilee, Jesus directed his ministry toward those persons rejected by organized religion, and neglected by society. Yet, this Galilean carpenter who walked with society's outcasts proceeds from the countryside toward Jerusalem, instructing people along the way about their oppression and turning away from God. Directing attention to the kingdom (realm) of God at hand.[286]

The attempt in *association* is to arrive at a comprehension of what Carl Raschke has referred to as a unity-behind-the-diversity approach, which is widely held among scholars and lay people.[287]   Professor John Macquarrie of Oxford University offered one clear expression of this perspective. Taking a philosophical approach, Macquarrie saw the riddle of religious pluralism as analogous to the age-old debate about "the one and the many," an argument that goes back at least to the ancient Greeks. "God," for Macquarrie, is the name of the ultimate unity beyond all seeming contradictions and differences. He wrote:

> These religions will be living side by side on earth in the foreseeable future.   They must seek to draw more closely together and demonstrate by common life and action their fundamental commitment to the One, however that One may be named in each religion... No single faith has yet attained to the understanding of the fullness of the One... Therefore each faith must be respectful and ready to learn from the spiritual insights of others.[288]

Raschke describes this as the "Hindu solution" to the question of pluralism. It claims, in effect, that the variegation in religious traditions is only a secondary quality, that underneath, all the separate rivers and rivulets of faith draw on a single mighty reservoir.   All the gods are avatars of the divine reality.[289]

This emphasizes God's embrace of all nations of people. God speaks to and acts for humanity through those who were considered foreigners or strangers – a Moabite woman becomes the ancestral mother of Jesus; a Syrophoenician woman expands Jesus' vision of his mission; a Roman centurion becomes an example of faithfulness. A list of these surprising agents of God could be lengthy. The paradigmatic embrace of all nations, however, occurred at Pentecost when Jews from all the known nations of the world heard in their own tongues the Galilean disciples praising God. Some years later Paul the apostle would dramatize the "strangeness" of that new experience of community in his description of the relationship of the Jews and Gentiles in the Corinthian congregation as "members of one another."[290]

The nature the church, the very essence of Christianity, is the movement towards radically inclusive community. Christ and his ministry modeled what it means for the church to be universal in its perspective (globality), catholic in its spirit, yet inclusive in its practice of community-building.

Christ is our peace, and the unity that he offers is clearly expressed in the song:

Blest be the tie that binds
our hearts in Christian love;
The fellowship of kindred minds
is like to that above.
Before our Father's throne
we pour our ardent prayers;
Our fears, our hopes, our aims are one,
our comforts and our cares.[291]

All persons are invited to join in the work of building radically inclusive community. We cannot live or grow without associating with one another in community, for in a world of interdependence, community extends to the farthest shores of our imaginations. In community we learn the both/and lessons of living. In community, we learn that survival does not belong merely to the "fittest" (understood as being the "most powerful"). Survival is about learning how to fit into our community and how the community fits us.[292]

On an individual level, it is important to understand that persons are affected by association across cultures. A comprehension of what Ewert Cousins, in *Christ of the 21st Century*, referred to as "a new global consciousness" might be helpful in better understanding and actualizing human association, community, and peacemaking, given the degree of human suffering and disintegration experienced among many persons throughout the world.[293]

The understandings of God, culture, humanity, and the positive or negative meanings that are given to the various differences among persons are shaped or constructed within the context of particular webs of "social relationships." They are not fixed in stone, but rather are influenced by and influence these particular relationships. This is the primary assumption from which the subject of multiculturalism has been approached, and is formally known as the theory of *social construction*. Social construction theory seeks to examine the development of jointly constructed understandings of the world that form the basis for shared assumptions about reality. Joan M. Martin posits that social construction theory allows her to keep her faith rooted in the realities of this world. For her, spiritual realities are rooted in everyday life.[294]

The creation of space for association and the free interchange of thoughts, feelings and beliefs among persons with different views, perspectives and backgrounds is critical in the process of developing radically inclusive community. Eric Law refers to this process as *dialogue*.[295] Dialogue is the meeting with the other person, the other group, the other people which confirms in its otherness, yet does not deny oneself and the ground on which it stands. The choice is not between oneself and the other, nor is there some objective ground to which one can rise above the facing sides, the conflicting claims. Rather, genuine dialogue is at once a confirmation of otherness and togetherness – the living embodiment of the biblical creation in which persons are really free, yet remain bound in relation with God. In genuine dialogue, each of the partners, even when standing in opposition to the other, heeds, affirms and confirms the opponent as an existing other.

Charles Foster, in *Embracing Diversity,* speaks of *association* in terms of the ways in which we might embrace strangers:

> The challenge of embracing the strangers we meet in our communities and congregations does not occur in the abstract. It emerges from the interactions of people from diverse cultural groups in the daily comings and goings of our life and work together.[296]

Foster goes on to point out how he became personally aware of the challenge of embracing strangers:

> This challenge was underscored for me during a conversation with a pastor serving a congregation of people whose ancestries could be traced back through the European immigration and the African Diaspora, and people who had recently come to the United States from thirteen different nations in Africa, Europe, the Caribbean, South America, the South Pacific, and Asia. Although the children and grandchildren of many long-time members visit from time to time, the congregation has only five three-generation families – three with European ancestries and two from Liberia. That is to

say that the ties contributing to the ethos in this congregation do not rely on the bonds of kinship.[297]

Indian Catholic Raimundo Panikkar, a priest and mystic whose father was a Hindu and whose mother was a Spanish Roman Catholic, pointed out that most dialogues between religious persons go astray when the participants begin advocating, comparing, defending, conceding – like diplomats negotiating a treaty. What Panikkar yearned for is more respect for silence, more shared awe and ecstasy. (This is a dialogue that draws partners into the "unspoken center" they share). One neither hides the differences nor trumpets the similarities, but allows both to be what they are. One waits and listens. The procedure is a nonviolent one, reminiscent of Gandhi's *ahimsa*.[298]

Thomas Merton pointed out that the test of our sincerity in human association in the practice of nonviolence and movement toward radically inclusive community is: *"are we willing to learn something from our adversaries?"*[299] If a new truth is made known, will we accept it? The dread of being open to the ideas of others generally comes from our hidden insecurity about our own convictions. We fear that we may be "converted" – or perverted – by a pernicious doctrine. On the other hand, if we are mature and objective in our open-mindedness, we may find that in viewing things from a basically different perspective we discover our own truth in a new light and are able to understand our own ideals more realistically.

5. Articulation

The development of radically inclusive community insists upon the consistent articulation of the meanings of the various symbols and practices that become a part of the new cultural reality. Human articulation is inescapably subjective, and yet therein lies a part of the value of cultural understanding through *articulation*. As a result of the subjective nature of *articulation,* our understanding only has tentative authority. This, however, does not diminish the value of *articulation*.

It was in the book *Footprints of a Dream* that Howard Thurman told the story of co-founding and pastoring the Church for the Fellowship of All Peoples in San Francisco. Thurman offered a complete and intimate picture of the beginnings of Fellowship Church, its early challenges, experiments, successful attainment of interracial unity in the 1940's and 50's, and ways that that congregation sought to articulate among themselves what effect the experiment in fellowship and radical inclusivity had on them. He described the everyday events of church life - worship services, choir practices, church school, etc. - against the backdrop of how they worked at becoming a multiracial, multi-class, multi-generational, multi-national congregation.[300]

The process of *articulation* helps us to move with hope and joy from those perspectives perhaps long held, and yet too partisan. Walter Brueggemann suggests that we may learn from the rabbis the marvelous rhythm of deep interpretive dispute and profound common yielding in joy and affectionate well-being. The characteristic and sometimes demonic mode of (some) interpretation is not tentativeness and relinquishment, but tentativeness hardening into absoluteness.[301]

Ewert Cousins offered a framework for articulating religion – particularly Christian faith – within the context of the broadening socio-cultural, postmodern realities of the new millennium. Christ is understood within the context of culture, and is to be understood within the fabric of all that comprises human life. Religion has typically reflected and often contributed to what occurs in society. The paradoxical nature of religion is that it is often directly or indirectly complicit in both the good and evil that exists in society.[302]

Religion is to be viewed as a process, and must now be understood in global context. It is no longer an option to confine religious thinking and practice to narrow and particular cultural contexts. In postmodernity, cultures are brought into closer contact by technology.[303] Cousins offered the illustration of an astronaut who travels into space for the first time, and looks down upon the earth. The astronaut is overwhelmed with what they see, as they now view the earth from a new and broader perspective. Likewise, a new global reality causes us to view the world from a different (perhaps broader) perspective.[304]

The result is the emergence of a global reality where it is now possible to comprehend diversity in the midst of unity. Cousins referred to this as the whole of "global consciousness."[305] This global consciousness will significantly impact religion in that there will be a more pronounced and intense meeting of world religions in the years to come. Currently, the impact of this global consciousness on religion can be seen in an increasing secularization of modern culture. In the future this secularization will result in an "emptying of heritage." [306]

6. Aspiration

In order to move toward the realization of radically inclusive community, processes of *aspiration* pertaining to the specific nature of ministry and the form(s) that ministry might take for the particular individual and ministry context should be undertaken. Howard Thurman intimated that "a dream is the bearer of new possibility, the enlarged horizon, the great hope."

As a part of the aspirational process, religious communities might engage in exploring questions such as, "What are we beginning to dream, envision, see and imagine as to God's preferred future for us in light of our shared gifts, graces and passions? What specific shape is our ministry as radically inclusive community taking? What risks are we willing to take to realize God's vision for our ministry, and for the church and world?" *Aspiration* is closely tied to imagination.

Walter Brueggemann, in *The Prophetic Imagination* offers this perspective:

> I understand imagination is no doubt a complex epistemological process, to be the capacity to entertain images of meaning and reality that are beyond the givens of observable experience. That is, imagination is the hosting of the "otherwise"... beyond the evident. Without that we have nothing to say. We must take risks and act daringly to push beyond what is known to that which is hoped for and trusted, but not yet in hand.[307]

In the *Mood of Christmas*, Thurman also offered a perspective on imagination:

> Imagination is the creative vehicle that carries one spirit into the dwelling place of another. There could be no sympathy in the world if (people) had not the gift of imagination. The spirit of man could never take flight in dreams, hopes, or aspirations if there were no wings of imaginations given as part of man's equipment for life.[308]

Today, there is a need to recapture the ancient wisdom of community-building, and to create new avenues of radically inclusive community. Langston Hughes wrote imaginatively of a world of such inclusivity in a poem:

> I dream a world where man
> No other man will scorn,
> Where love will bless the earth
> And peace its paths adorn.
> I dream a world where all
> Will know sweet freedom's way,
> Where greed no longer saps the soul
> Nor avarice blights the day
> A world I dream where black and white
> Whatever race you be,
> Will share the bounties of the earth
> And every man is free,
> Where wretchedness will hang its head
> And joy, like a pearl
> Attends the needs of all mankind –
> Of such I dream my world![309]

Aspiration helps to draw upon the creative gifts that persons have been given by God in the movement toward developing radically inclusive community. This might be referred to as the "jazz" of becoming community – the improvisational, creative and extemporaneous processes which can result in significant breakthroughs. *Aspiration* speaks to the freedom and creative capacity that persons possess individually and collectively. It involves the capacity to see old things in new ways, to forge and create something viable from that which doesn't exist or has lost its vitality. It empowers us to think and create in terms that reinforce personal sanctity, identity and the value of all persons, and ultimately to facilitate the creation of new shapes and forms of being community.

Here, additional questions that might be explored are, "What innovative and creative approaches might be undertaken in community-building? What gifts and agency has God placed in and among people in community (music, dance, poetry, drama, literature, liturgy, prayer, technology, capacity-building, consensus-building, etc.) that might make for the movement towards radically inclusive community?"

7. Anticipation

Anticipation involves further capturing and embracing a bold vision and holy imagination as to what a preferred, better future might entail. Howard Thurman pointed out that we are accustomed to thinking of imagination as a useful tool in the hands of the artist as the reproduce in varied forms that which they see beyond the rim of fact that encircles them. There are times when the imagination is regarded as a delightful and often whimsical characteristic of what we are pleased to call the "childish mind."[310]

Thurman went on to speak of the place of imagination in human relationships. He intimated that the place where imagination shows its greatest powers as the *angelos* of God is in the miracle which it creates when one person, standing in place, is able, while remaining there, to put oneself in another's place. To send their imagination forth to establish a beachhead in another person's spirit, and from that vantage point so to blend with the other's landscape that what they see and feel is authentic – this is the great adventure of human relations. But this is not enough. The imagination must report its findings accurately without regard to all prejudgments, and private or collective fears. But this is not enough. There must be both a spontaneous and a calculating response to such knowledge which will result in sharing of resources at their deepest level.[311]

Further, Thurman asserted that without *anticipation,* human love would be impossible to achieve for there can be no love among human beings where there is no power of self-projection. The mechanism of love is the ability to put oneself in the life of another and to look upon the world through the other's eyes – to enter into the feeling, thinking and reacting of another, even as one remains oneself...*(Anticipation)* is the creative vehicle that carries one spirit into the dwelling place of another. There could be no sympathy in the world if persons had not the gift of *anticipation.* The spirit of humanity could never take flight in dreams, hopes or imagination if there were no wings of *aspiration* given as a part of humanity's equipment for life.[312]

Anticipation leads us to dream and envision the possibilities of radically inclusive community among the people of God. The scripture offers that "where there is no vision, the people cast off restraint" (Proverbs 29:18). The Prophet Joel's eschatological and aspirational vision anticipates the possibilities of God's presence as people look to the future with hope:

> "In the last day, I (God) will pour out my spirit on all flesh, and your sons and daughters shall prophecy, and the old shall dream dreams and the young shall see visions" (Joel 2:28).

Furthermore, the Prophet Jeremiah articulated God's vision for humanity –

"I know the plans I have for you", says the Lord, "plans not to harm you, but plans for your well-being (shalom), plans to give you a future with hope" (Jeremiah 29:11).

Thurman helps us to see that we need to take an anticipatory and imaginative look toward a fresh and generous ideal of radical inclusivity for all humanity. Christian humility and hope are inseparable within the context of community building. The quality of inclusivity is predicated largely on the purity of the Christian hope and imagination behind it. The Christian knows that there are radically sound possibilities in everyone, and believes that love, grace and mercy always have the power to bring out those possibilities at the most unexpected moments. Therefore, if one has hope that God will bring forth unity to the world, it is because one also trusts that humanity, God's creation, is not basically evil, that there is in us a potentiality for peace and order which can be realized, provided the right conditions exist. Christians will do their part in creating these conditions by preferring love and trust over hate and suspiciousness. Obviously, once again, this "hope in humankind" must not be naïve. But experience itself has shown, in the last few years, how much an attitude of simplicity and openness can do to break down barriers of suspicion that have divided people for centuries.[313]

In the new millennium, it is important to creatively imaginatively and hopefully apply the wisdom of nonviolence to politics, economics and science. For many in the West, increased materialism and unprecedented consumerism have not led to inner peace or happiness. Although technology has afforded us many benefits, it has not helped us distinguish between what enhances life and humanity, and what destroys life and humanity. As we look to the future, we must look with aspiration and hope at ways that we might use all of our gifts and agency to foster radically inclusive community.

8. Appropriation

In the final analysis, Howard Thurman viewed community as a transformational process that needed to be understood within the context of the salvation of individuals and the community itself. The development of radically inclusive community thus requires God-connectedness through the inspiration of the Holy Spirit. As God inspires persons, peace and reconciliation will become the reality that ultimately leads to radically inclusive community.

For the church, the *appropriation* of community as a transformational Christ-centered, Spirit-filled process can be understood within the context of God's ongoing work in salvation history. Again, an imitation of the unconditional love revealed in the life and teachings of Jesus can be helpful in the quest for radically inclusive community. Moving toward a deeper sense of who we are as individuals and community will enable us to live more shalom-filled lives, modeled on the life of Christ. There is the obligation to treat every person as Christ Himself, respecting her/his life as if it were the life of Christ.

Thurman held to a vision of humanity as radically inclusive community. For him, the key to overcoming social disintegration and developing such community is the actualization of *agape*. *Agape* involves the recognition that in God's divine and unconditional love, God created humanity in God's image, and that all human life is of sacred worth and is interrelated. Thurman asserted that humanity must be seen as a single process. All persons belong to the family of God and therefore whatever directly affects one person affects all indirectly.[314]   For example, Thurman recognized that not only did the American slavery of blacks adversely affect the freedom of white labor, which had to bargain from the depressed economic base imposed by slavery, but also *de facto* discrimination affects poor whites that have to exist within the same economic confines as poor blacks.

Appropriation can be helpful in resolving difficult philosophical, ideological and sociopolitical issues today. Thurman tried to avoid extremes, and sought to arrive at the synthesis that combined aspects of multiple converging realities.   He avoided extreme "either-or" viewpoints about black and white, rich and poor, materialism and humanism, pessimism and optimism, communism and capitalism, liberalism and conservatism. Instead of "either-or" viewpoints, he sought "both-and" solutions by combining conflicting prospects to create a greater, more harmonious whole - a synthesis.

Racial reconciliation was one form of synthesis championed by Thurman as a solution to racial conflict and other forms of social disintegration.   Racial reconciliation, leading to the development of radically inclusive community was ultimately embodied and exemplified his synthetic and integrative approach.

Radically inclusive community includes persons of different races, sexes, ages, religions, cultures, viewpoints, lifestyles, and stages of development, and serves to move humanity into a whole that is greater – more actualized and dynamic – than the sum of its parts.

For Thurman, the promise of radically inclusive community is at the heart of Christ's work; in him human beings are children of God, and kindred with one another. The church, the community of those who confess Christ as Lord, is an embodiment of unity within history. For this reason, the church must help the world to see and achieve community, while knowing that unity among human beings is possible only if there is real justice for all persons.

Concluding Thoughts

In order to bring the significance of Howard Thurman's life, theology and ministry into contemporary perspective, it is necessary to have a clear picture of his pastoral-prophetic identity in light of his persistent yearning to appropriate radically inclusive community. It has been my attempt in this volume to demonstrate that Thurman's theoretical and praxiological approach to ministry – within the context of the Christian love-ethic - can serve as a means of explicating and applying the principle elements involved in becoming radically inclusive community in the 21st century and beyond.

Clearly, Thurman was a Christian minister who believed in God, accepted the Christian account of the historical Jesus as a key to a full and necessary understanding of God's work in history, and insisted on the meaningful appropriation of radically inclusive community. Thurman viewed the kin-dom of God as a communal expression of God's will, which was revealed in the life and mission of Jesus of Nazareth who was invariably for and with the "disinherited". Though a Christian, Thurman often sought to comprehend the divine love and will of God in Christ within the context of prophetic expressions outside the norms of traditional Christianity. In these interreligious expressions, Thurman saw the hand of God seeking to pull humanity - in all its rich diversity, dreams, fears and hopes - into vitality and harmony.

The eight principles that have been offered as a culmination of this study reflect the common appropriation of the Christian spirituality – a spiritual theology - of Thurman as a foundation for spiritual and social transformation. For Thurman, spirituality found its origins and coherence in the Black church, along with family (nuclear and extended) and community structures of the American South of the first quarter of the 20th century.

Through his analysis and appropriation of various strands of theological, philosophical and socio-political thinking, Thurman sought to synthesize and articulate the relationship among love, justice, forgiveness, righteousness and power, with particular focus on the eradication of oppression on the basis of race, class, and other aspects of social distinction in the American churches and society of his day. His persistent objective was to raise the consciousness of society and the church, and to move the nation and the world toward the actualization of radically inclusive community.

In the final analysis, Howard Thurman went to great lengths to explicate the quality of whole-hearted, profound Christian love, which can and must be the substance uniting all humanity into a common bond of sisters and brothers, showing forth in all human relationships, and ultimately expressed in radically inclusive community.

ENDNOTES

Chapter One Notes

[1]Howard Thurman, *With Head and Heart - The Autobiography of Howard Thurman* (New York: Harcourt Brace & Company, 1979), 6.

[2] Ibid., 16ff.

[3] Ibid., 24.

[4] Alton B. Pollard, *Mysticism and Social Change: The Social Witness of Howard Thurman,* (New York: Peter Lang, 1992), 3.

[5] Michael I. N. Dash, et. al. *Hidden Wholeness: An African American Spirituality for Individuals and Communities* (Cleveland, OH: United Church Press), 1.

[6] Howard Thurman, *For the Inward Journey* (Richmond, IN: Friend United Press, 1984), x.

[7] Mozella Gordon Mitchell, *Spiritual Dynamics of Howard Thurman* (Bristol, IN: Wyndham Hall Press, 1985), 105. Alton Pollard also offers an exposition on this point in *Mysticism and Social Change,* 46.

[8] Luther E. Smith, *Howard Thurman: The Mystic as Prophet* (Richmond, Indiana: Friends United Press, 1992), see pp. 15-20.

[9] Ibid. Smith offers an explication on these four major influences in *Howard Thurman: The Mystic as Prophet.*

[10] Roberta Byrd Barr, interview with Howard Thurman, Seattle, Washington, January 1969.

[11] Wayne A. Meeks, *The Writings of St. Paul* (New York: Norton, 1978), xiv.

[12] Mary E. Goodwin, "Racial Roots and Religion: An Interview with Howard Thurman," *Christian Century,* 9 May 1973, 534.

[13] Ibid.

[14] Ibid., 533.

[15] Elizabeth Yates, *Howard Thurman: Portrait of a Practical Dreamer* (New York: John Day, 1964), 23.

[16] Ibid., pp. 47-48.

[17] Smith, 138, see also Howard Thurman, *Deep is the Hunger: Meditations of Apostles of Sensitiveness* (New York: Harper and Brothers, 1951), pp. 10-11.

[18] Ibid.

[19] Ibid., pp. 23-24.

[20] George Cross, *What is Christianity? - A Study of Rival Interpretations* (Chicago: University of Chicago Press, 1918), 187.

[21] Ibid., 193.

[22] George Cross, *Christian Salvation: A Modern Interpretation* (Chicago: University of Chicago Press, 1925), 133.

[23] Ibid., 33.

[24] Henry Robins believed that Christianity had the "Supreme Pattern" of the moral personality in the "Lord Jesus Christ." This view was explicated in his *Four Addresses Before the Burma Baptist Mission Conference* (Rangoon: American Baptist Mission Press, 1928).

[25] Both Henry Robins and George Cross defined "saved community" within the context of an environment of the growth of personality.

[26] Smith, 32. Smith recounts Thurman's views on Henry Robins from a 1978 personal interview.

[27] Pollard, 33. Pollard makes reference here to Howard Thurman, "Mysticism and Social Change", a 15–part lecture series delivered at the Pacific School of Religion, Berkley, CA, July 5-28, 1978.

[28] Ibid., 33.

[29] Smith, 33.

[30] Howard Thurman, *Mysticism and the Experience of Love* (Wallingford, PA: Pendle Hill, 1961), pp. 4-5.

[31] Kenneth Cauthen, *The Impact of American Religious Liberalism* (New York: Harper and Row, 1962), pp. 27-28.

[32] Smith, 93.

[33] Reinhold Niebuhr, *Moral Man and Immoral Society* (New York: Scribner, 1933), pp. xxii-xxiii.

[34] Smith, 146. Based on Luther Smith's personal interview with Thurman.

[35] Niebuhr, *Moral Man,* pp. 249 and 273.

[36] Reinhold Niebuhr, *An Interpretation of Christian Ethics* (New York: Harper and Brothers, 1935), 140.

[37] Mitchell, 52.

[38] Walter Earl Fluker. *They Looked For a City: A Comparative Analysis of the Ideal of Community in the Thought of Howard Thurman and Martin Luther King, Jr.* (New York: University Press of America, 1989), 174.

[39] Lerone Bennett, Jr. "Eulogy of Howard Thurman: Tributes to Genius," *The African American Pulpit*, Valley Forge, PA: Judson Press, Winter 2001, 63. Bennett made reference to Thurman's perspective on life and personal identity at Thurman's funeral in 1981.

[40] Luther Smith and Alton Pollard are two of the scholars who have placed Thurman within the historical context of the mystical tradition.

[41] Pollard, 1.

[42] Cheslyn Jones, Jeffrey Wainwright and Edward Yarnold, SJ, eds. *The Study of Spirituality* (Oxford, UK: Oxford University Press, 1986), 19.

[43] This prayer by Howard Thurman appears in the *United Methodist Hymnal* (Nashville: United Methodist Publishing, 1989), 401.

[44] Howard Thurman, *Disciplines of the Spirit* (Richmond, IN: Friends United Press, 1987), 9.

[45] Howard Thurman, *Deep River and the Negro Spiritual Speaks of Life and Death* (Richmond, IN: Friends United Press, 1975), Thurman's thoughts on the river as metaphor for life and meaning is explicated throughout.

[46] Howard Thurman, *For the Inward Journey* (Richmond, IN: Friends United Press, 1984), 64.

[47] Howard Thurman, *Meditations of the Heart* (Richmond, IN: Friends United Press, 1953), 15.

[48] Smith, 15.

[49] Howard Thurman, "Mysticism and Social Action," *Eden Theological Seminary Bulletin* IV (Spring Quarter, 1939): 27.

[50] Ibid.

[51] Smith, 17.

[52] Segundo Galilea, "Liberation as an Encounter with Politics and Contemplation," in *The Mystical and Political Dimension of the Christian Faith,* eds. Claude Gaffre and Gustavo Gutierrez (New York: Herder and Herder, 1974), 28.

[53] Ibid., pp. 31-32.

[54] Pollard, 34.

[55] Ibid., 1.

[56] Ibid.

[57] Jessie L. Jackson interview by Madison Davis Lacey, Jr. and Henry Hampton "Eyes on the Prize II Interviews" (St. Louis, MO: Washington University, April 11, 1989), http://digital.wustl.edu/e/eii/eiiweb/jac5427.0519.072marc_record_interviewer_process.html.

[58] Pollard, pp. 7-8.

[59] Ibid., 10.

[60] Walter Brueggemann, *The Prophetic Imagination* (Philadelphia: Fortress Press, 1978), 111.

[61] See Smith. pp. 15-20.

[62] Howard Thurman, *Essential Writings* (Maryknoll, NY: Orbis Press, 2006), 46.

Chapter Two Notes

[63] Sudarshan Kapur, *Raising Up a Prophet: The African-American Encounter with Gandhi* (Boston: Beacon Press, 1992), see pp. 81-100. Also, Thurman discusses his encounter with Gandhi in *With Head and Heart*, pp. 130-35.

[64] See Thomas Merton, *Gandhi on Nonviolence* (New York: New Directions, 1964). Merton offers details on the life of Mohandas Gandhi.

[65] Ibid.

[66] Ibid.

[67] John Dear, "The Experiments of Gandhi: Nonviolence in the Nuclear Age," *Fellowship* (New York: Fellowship of Reconciliation, January/February, 1988).

[68] J. Deotis Roberts, "Gandhi and King: On Conflict Resolution," in *Shalom Papers: A Journal of Theology and Public Policy,* ed. Victoria J. Barnett (Washington, DC: Church's Center for Theology and Public Policy, Vol. 11, No. 2, Spring 2000), 36.

[69] Rajmohan Gandhi, "Gandhi's Unfulfilled Legacy: Prospects for Reconciliation in Racial/Ethnic Conflict" (1995 Cynthia Wedel Lecture, Church's Center for Theology and Public Policy, Wesley Theological Seminary, Washington, DC, April 27, 1995). In this lecture, Rajmohan Gandhi offers a view of Mohandas Gandhi's life and unfinished legacy from the perspective of a contemporary Indian scholar.

[70] Ibid.

[71] Ibid.

[72] Ibid.

[73] William Shannon, *Seeds of Peace: Contemplation and Non-Violence* (New York: Crossroad Publishing, 1996), 154.

[74] Ibid., 153.

[75] See Thomas Merton, *Gandhi on Nonviolence,* for details on Gandhi's development of the conceptualization of *Satyagraha.*

[76] Roberts, 37.

[77] Ibid.

[78] See Mohandas K. Gandhi, "Nonviolence – the Greatest Force," in *The World Tomorrow,* (October 1926).

[79] Dear.

[80] Ibid.

[81] Ibid.

[82] Mohandas Gandhi, "Seven Social Sins", Gandhi first published this list in his weekly newspaper *Young India* on October 22, 1925.

[83] Jim Wallis, *The Soul of Politics* (New York: The New Press, 1994), xiii.

[84] Shannon, 154.

[85] Ibid.

[86] Mairead Corrigan Maguire, "Gandhi and the Ancient Wisdom of Nonviolence," *Fellowship* (New York: Fellowship of Reconciliation, June 1988).

[87] Dear.

[88] Shannon, 154.

[89] See Gandhi, "Nonviolence – The Greatest Force", 124.

[90] Ibid.

[91] Ibid.

[92] See, Yates, pp. 104-109.

[93] Ibid, Yates. 95.

[94] Howard Thurman, *Footprints of a Dream: The Dawn of the Idea of the Church for the Fellowship of All Peoples: Letters Between Alfred Fisk and Howard Thurman, 1943-1944,* (San Francisco: Lawton and Alfred Kennedy, 1975), 24.

[95] Ibid.

[96] Ibid.

[97] Thurman, *With Head and Heart,* 132.

[98] Roberts, 32.

[99] Gandhi, "Nonviolence – The Greatest Force," 124.

[100] Ibid., 121.

[101] Ibid., 123.

[102] Gandhi, "Nonviolence – The Greatest Force," 123. Mrs. Sue Bailey Thurman's response fits with the conceptualization of the "moral suasion" as discussed by J. Deotis Roberts. See, Roberts, "Moral Suasion as Non-violent Direct Action," *Journal for Religious Thought* (Vol. 35, No. 2, Fall /Winter 1978-79), see pp. 29-43.

[103]Walter E. Fluker and Catherine Tumber eds. *A Strange Freedom: The Best of Howard Thurman on Religious Experience and Public Life* (Boston: Beacon Books, 1998), 7.

[104] Pollard, 37.

[105] Ibid.

[106] Gandhi, "Nonviolence – The Greatest Force", 105-106.

[107] Pollard, 23.

[108] Ibid., 38. Pollard here makes reference to Thurman's essay "The Fascist Masquerade" which appears as Chapter 4 in *The Church and Organized Movements,* ed. Randolph C. Miller (New York: Harper Brothers, 1946), see pp. 82-100.

[109] Smith, 9.

[110] Thomas Merton, "Blessed are the Meek" in *The Nonviolent Alternative (*Revised edition of *Thomas Merton on Peace).* New York: Farrar, Straus and Giroux, 1980.

[111] Ibid.

Chapter Three Notes

[112] Smith, 107.

[113] Ibid., 62.

[114] See Howard Thurman, *Jesus and the Disinherited,* (Richmond, IN: Friends United Press, 1969), 89-109.

[115] Olin Moyd, *Sacred Art, Sacred Art: Preaching and Theology in the African American Tradition* (Valley Forge, PA: Judson Press, 1995, 22.

[116] Thurman, *Jesus and the Disinherited,* 11.

[117] Ibid., 21.

[118] John J. Ansbro, *Martin Luther King, Jr.: Nonviolent Tactics and Strategies for Social Change* (Maryknoll, NY: Orbis Books, 2000), 27.

[119] Thurman, *Jesus and the Disinherited,* 89.

[120] Ansbro, 28.

[121] Thurman, *Jesus and the Disinherited,* 93-94.

[122] Ibid., pp. 94-95.

[123] Ibid., pp. 104-105.

[124] Greg Moses, *Revolution of Conscience: Martin Luther King, Jr. and the Philosophy of Nonviolence* (New York: Guilford Press, 1997), 151.

[125] Thurman, *Jesus and the Disinherited,* 50ff.

[126] Thurman, *Disciplines of the Spirit,* 122.

[127] Howard Thurman, *Deep is the Hunger,* 109.

[128] Luther Smith, 50.

[129] Howard Thurman, *The Mood of Christmas* (Richmond, IN: Friends United Press, 1969), 12.

[130] Ibid., 11.

[131] Ibid., 10.

[132] Dietrich Bonhoeffer, *Meditations on the Cross* (Louisville, KY: Westminster John Knox Press, 1996), 64.

[133] Ibid., 76.

[134] Thurman, *The Negro Spiritual Speaks of Life and Death*, pp. 13-14.

[135] James Cone, *The Cross and the Lynching Tree* (New York: Orbis Books, 2015), 160.

[136] Ibid.

[137] Ibid., xv.

[138] Kelly Brown Douglas, *Stand Your Ground: Black Bodies and the Justice of God* (Maryknoll, NY: Orbis Books, 2015), 170.

[139] Obery Hendricks, *The Politics of Jesus: Rediscovering the Revolutionary Nature of Jesus' Teachings and How They Have Been Corrupted* (New York: Doubleday, 2006), 5.

[140] See Hendricks, *The Politics of Jesus.* The principles are outlined and explicated upon throughout this book.

[141] Thurman, *Jesus and the Disinherited*, 89.

[142] Smith, 48.

[143] Thurman, *Disciplines of the Spirit,* pp. 104-105.

[144] Smith, 107.

[144] Thurman, *Jesus and the Disinherited*, 89.

[144] Smith, 48.

[145] Ibid.

[146] Thurman, *Jesus and the Disinherited,* 74.

[147] See Howard Thurman's analysis of hate (hatred) in *Jesus and the Disinherited,* pp. 77-78.

[148] Ibid.

[149] Ibid., pp. 89-90.

[150] Thurman, *The Mood of Christmas*, 19.

[151] Ibid., 51.

[152] Ibid., 9.

[153] See Alonzo Johnson, *Good News for the Disinherited: Howard Thurman on Jesus of Nazareth and Human Liberation* (New York: University Press of America, 1997). Johnson provides a detailed treatment and explication of Thurman's Christology, with liberation as the defining motif of Christ's mission and ministry.

[154] See Thurman, *Deep River and the Negro Spiritual Speaks of Life and Death.* Throughout, Thurman explicates the role of the spiritual and other expressions of black religion as means of survival for slaves.

[155] Thurman, *The Mood of Christmas,* 9.

Chapter Four Notes

[156] Thurman, *The Mood of Christmas,* 122.

[157] Thurman, *Deep is the Hunger,* 109.

[158] Smith, 50.

[159] Thurman, *The Mood of Christmas,* 63.

[160] Thurman, *Disciplines of the Spirit,* 105.

[161] Howard Thurman, *The Search for Common Ground: An Inquiry into the Basis of Man's Experience of Community* (Richmond, Indiana: Friends United Press, 1971), 6.

[162] See Thurman, *Disciplines of the Spirit,* pp. 104-127.

[163] Thurman, *The Search for Common Ground,* 104.

[164] Howard Thurman, *Disciplines of the Spirit,* 113.

[165] Ibid., 114.

[166] Ibid., see pp. 48-55.

[167] Ibid., see pp. 55-62.

[168] Ibid., 88.

[169] Ibid, 103.

[170] Ibid., 97.

[171] Lerone Bennett, Jr., "Eulogy of Howard Thurman: Tributes to Genius", in *The African American Pulpit* (Valley Forge, PA: Judson Press, 2001), p. 63.

[172] Jim Wallis *America's Original Sin: Racism, White Privilege and the Bridge to a New America* (Grand Rapids, MI: Brazos Press, 2017), 102.

[173] Smith, 202.

[174] See Thurman, *Jesus and the Disinherited*, pp. 11-35.

[175] Thurman, *Jesus and the Disinherited*, 50ff.

[176] Smith, 133. Smith makes reference to Thurman's "Peace Tactics and a Racial Minority," *The World Tomorrow,* December, 1928, pp. 505-507.

[177] Smith, 107.

[178] George D. Kelsey, *Racism and the Christian Understanding of Man* (Eugene , OR: Wipf an Stock Publishers, 1965), 9.

[179] Ibid., 92.

[180] Pollard, 6. Pollard makes reference to the work to this effect by Vincent Harding, C. Eric Lincoln, and Gayraud Wilmore.

[181] Ibid.

[182] See Thurman, *Jesus and the Disinherited,* pp. 89-109.

[183] See Kipton Jensen and Preston King, "Beloved Community: Martin Luther King, Howard Thurman and Josiah Royce" (Atlanta: Morehouse Faculty Publication, #23, 2017).

[184] Abraham Joshua Heschel, "The Reason for my Involvement in the Peace Movement" (first written and delivered in 1972), included in *Moral Grandeur and Spiritual Audacity*, Susannah Heschel, ed. (New York: Farrar, Straus and Giroux, 1997).

[185] See James Cone, "Theology's Great Sin: Silence in the Face of White Supremacy" in *Black Theology, 2:2* (Maryknoll, NY: Orbis, 2004), 139-152, footnote 1.

[186] Garth Baker-Fletcher, *Somebodyness: Martin Luther King, Jr. and the Theory of Dignity.* (Minneapolis, MN: Fortress Press, 1993, 132.

[187] See Thurman, *Disciplines of the Spirit,* pp. 111-21, and Alton Pollard, *Mysticism and Social Change,* 109.

[188] Thurman, *Disciplines of the Spirit,* 113.

[189] See Smith, Chapter 4.

[190] Ibid.

[191] Lewis V. Baldwin, *There is a Balm in Gilead: The Cultural Roots of Martin Luther King, Jr.* (Minneapolis: Fortress Press, 1993), 65.

[192] Thurman, *Jesus and the Disinherited,* 109

[193] Ibid., 29.

[194] See Thurman, *Deep River and the Negro Spiritual Speaks of Life and Death* for an explication of Thurman's perspective on the Negro Spirituals as a primary source in nonviolent protest and survival for Blacks.

[195] See Thurman, *Deep River and the Negro Spiritual Speaks of Life and Death.* Thurman speaks of the place of the Negro Spiritual in community-building and in the inculcation of nonviolence and the Christian love ethic throughout this work.

[196] James Cone, *The Spirituals and the Blues* (Maryknoll, NY: Orbis Books, 1972), 16. Here Cone makes reference to Howard Thurman's thinking in *The Negro Spiritual Speaks of Life and Death,* see pp. 12-15.

[197] See Smith, *The Mystic as Prophet,* 116-117. Smith points out that Thurman's two books that give full treatment of Negro Spirituals are *Deep River* (1945) and *The Negro Spiritual Speaks of Life and Death* (1947). These works speak to the plight of black people and their quest for freedom as articulated through the Negro Spirituals.

[198] See Howard Thurman, "The Will To Segregate," *Fellowship* (New York: The Fellowship of Reconciliation, August, 1943).

[199] Ibid.

[200] Smith, 142.

Chapter Five Notes

[201] Smith, 107.
[202] Thurman, *With Head and Heart,* 144.
[203] Yates, 95.
[204] Thurman, *Footprints of a Dream*, 46.
[205] Ibid., 13.
[206] Mark L. Chapman, *Christianity on Trial: African-American Religious Thought Before and After Black Power* (Maryknoll, NY: Orbis Books, 1996), 28.
[207] Thurman, *Footprints of a Dream,* 65. Thurman's conception and practice of "church" is further developed in the works of Dennis Wiley, *The Concept of the Church in the Theology of Howard Thurman,* Ph.D. Dissertation (Union Theological Seminary, N.Y., 1988), and in Chapman, *Christianity on Trial.*
[208] Henry Nelson Wieman, *Methods of Private Religious Living* (New York: MacMillan Co., 1929), 140.
[209] Smith, 73.
[210] Howard Thurman, "The Fascist Masquerade" in *The Church and Organized Movements,* Chapter 4, ed. Randolph Crump Miller (New York: Harper and Brothers, 1946), pp. 82-100.
[211] Ibid.
[212] See Thurman, "The Will to Segregate."
[213] Ibid.
[214] Howard Thurman, *The Creative Encounter: An Interpretation of Religion and The Social Witness* (Richmond, IN: Friends United Press, 1954), pp. 140-145.
[215] Thurman, *Jesus and the Disinherited,* 98.
[216] Thurman, *The Search for Common Ground,* 103.
[217] Ibid., 104.
[218] Smith, 142.
[219] Thurman, *Footprints of a Dream*, 109.
[220] Pollard, 79.
[221] Smith, 11.

[222] Thurman, *With Head and Heart,* 142.

[223] "Fellowship Church History," The Church for the Fellowship of All Peoples, http://www.fellowship.org/history.html.

[224] Thurman, *With Head and Heart,* 142.

[225] Ibid., 144.

[226] Thurman, *Disciplines of the Spirit,* pp. 114-115.

[227] Wallis, *America's Original Sin,* 102.

Chapter Six Notes

[228] Fluker, 156.

[229] Smith, 49.

[230] Ibid.

[231] Ibid., 50.

[232] Smith, 54.

[233] Thurman, *Deep is the Hunger,* 62.

[234] Ibid., 63.

[235] Chapman, 28.

[236] Howard Thurman, *The Luminous Darkness,* (New York: Harper and Row, 1965), pp. 98-99.

[237] Thurman, *Deep River,* pp. 17-18.

[238] Thurman, *Disciplines of the Spirit,* pp, 104-105.

[239] Smith, 51.

[240] Thurman, *The Mood of Christmas,* 9.

[241] Thurman, *The Search for Common Ground,* 43.

[242] Martin E. Marty, *Pilgrims in Their Own Land: 500 Years of Religion in America* (New
York: Penguin Books, 1984), 75.

[243] Peter Paris, *The Social Teaching of the Black Churches,* (Minneapolis: Fortress Press, 1985, see chapter 5.

[244] Walter Rauschenbusch, *A Theology of the Social Gospel* (Louisville, KY:
Westminster John Knox Press, 1945), 1.

[245] Ibid.

[246] Martin Luther King, Jr., "A Knock at Midnight", *Strength to Love* (New York: Harper & Row, 1963), 57.

[247] Ibid., pp. 94-95.

[248] Jim Wallis, *On God's Side: What Religion Forgets and Politics Hasn't Learned about Serving the Common Good* (Grand Rapids, MI: Brazos Press, 2013), 109.

[249] Thurman, *The Search for Common Ground : An Inquiry into the Basis of Man's Experience of Community* (Richmond, Indiana: Friends United Press), pp. 2-3.

Chapter Seven Notes

[250] Lewis Brown Griggs and Lente-Louise Louw, *Valuing Diversity: New Tools for a New Reality,* (New York: McGraw Hill, 1995), 159.

[251] Wallis, *On God's Side*, see pp. 275-283.

[252] Griggs and Louw.

[253] Thurman, *The Creative Encounter,* 139.

[254] Thurman, *Jesus and the Disinherited,* 11.

[255] Michael Emerson and Smith, Christian, *Divided by Faith: Evangelical Religion and the Problem of Race,* Oxford, UK: Oxford University Press, 2000), 154f.

[256] Ibid.

[257] Ibid.

[258] See Eileen Guenther, *The American Organist*, November 2008. "From the President", vol. 42, no. 11.

Chapter Eight Notes

[259] Francis of Assisi, Italy, 13th Century, see *The United Methodist Hymnal* (Nashville, TN: United Methodist Publishing, 1989), 481. See also *St. Francis and the Foolishness of God* by Marie Dennis, et. al. (Maryknoll, NY: Orbis Books, 1997).

[260] See Thurman, *Deep is the Hunger,* pp. 51-52, and *Disciplines of the Spirit,* pp.111-121.

[261] Eric H.F. Law, *The Bush Was Burning, But Not Consumed* (St. Louis, MO: Chalice Press, 1996), 59

[262] See Milton J. Bennett, "A Developmental Approach to Training for Intercultural Sensitivity," in *Theories and Methods in Cross-Cultural Orientation,* ed. Judith N. Martin, International Journal of Intercultural Relations, Vol. 5, No. 2 (New York: Persimmon Press, 1986), pp. 179-196, and Milton J. Bennett, "Toward Ethnorelativism: A Developmental Model of Intercultural Sensitivity," in *Cross-Cultural Orientation*, ed. R. Michael Paige (Lanham, MD: University Press of America, 1986), pp. 46-69.

[263] Ibid.

[264] Thurman, *Disciplines of the Spirit*, 105.

[265] Thurman, *The Search for Common Ground,* 6.

[266] See Raleigh Washington and Glen Kehrein, *Breaking Down Walls: A Model for Reconciliation in an Age of Racial Strife* (Chicago: Moody, 1993), chapter 15, for a complete discussion of Washington and Kehrein's conception of "call."

[267] J. Philip Wogaman, *Christian Moral Judgment* (Louisville: Westminster/John Knox Press, 1989), Wogaman discusses the method of positive presumption on pages 89-115.

[268] Henry Mitchell and Nicholas Lewter-Cooper, *Soul Theology: The Heart of American Black Culture* (New York: Harper and Row, 1986), 95.

[269] Ibid., 96.

[270] Ibid.

[271] Merton, *The Nonviolent Alternative*, 112.

[272] Ibid.

[273] Ethnic Ministries, Board of Discipleship, *Ethnic Ministries in the United Methodist Church* (Nashville: Discipleship Resources, 1976), 1.

[274] Thurman, *With Head and Heart*, 142.

[275] Dietrich Bonhoeffer, *The Cost of Discipleship* (New York: Collier Books, 1949, First published in 1937), Throughout, Bonhoeffer elaborates on the distinction between "cheap grace" and "costly grace" within the context of Christian discipleship.

[276] Washington and Kehrein. Washington and Kehrein offer an in-depth analysis of *Intentionality* and *Sincerity* as two important practices in facilitating racial reconciliation at Rock of Our Salvation Church in Chicago, IL.

[277] Shannon, 126.

[278] Martin Luther King, Jr., *Where Do We Go from Here: Chaos or Community?* (New York: Harper & Row, 1967), 181.

[279] Gilbert H. Caldwell, *Race, Racism and Reconciliation* (Philadelphia: Simon Printing and Publishing, Inc., 1989), 32.

[280] Ibid., 34.

[281] Marjorie Thompson, *Soul Feast: An Invitation to the Christian Spiritual Life* (Louisville, KY; Westminster John Knox Press, 1995), 127.

[282] Pollard, *Mysticism and Social Change,* 95.

[283] Carlyle Fielding Stewart, "Comparative Analysis of Theological-Ontology and Ethical Method in the Theologies of James H. Cone and Howard Thurman," (Ph.D. dissertation, Northwestern University, 1982), 362-75.

[284] Smith, 117.

[285] Thurman, *The Search for Common Ground,* pp. 2-3.

[286] Harold Recinos, *Jesus Weeps* (Nashville: Abingdon Press, 1992), 45-46.

[287] See Harvey Cox, *Many Mansions: A Christian's Encounter with Other Faiths* (Boston: Beacon Press, 1988), 166ff. Cox discusses Carl Raschke's four typologies as an attempt at arriving at answers to the "truth question" among persons of diverse cultures and religions.

[288] See also John Macquarrie, *Christian Unity and Christian Diversity* (London: SCM Press, 1975), 167-168. Here Macquarrie offers a complete explication of the unity-diversity issue in religious perspective.
[289] Cox, 168.
[290] Charles Foster, *Embracing Diversity* (Washington, DC: The Alban Institute), 52.
[291] See the *United Methodist Hymnal* Nashville: United Methodist Publishing House, 1989), 557. Written by John Fawcett, 1782.
[292] Matthew Fox, *Creation Spirituality: Liberating Gifts for The Peoples of the Earth* (New York: HarperCollins, 1991), 50.
[293] Ewert Cousins, *Christ of the 21st Century* (New York: Continuum, 1998), pp. 2-3.
[294] Joan M. Martin, presentation at Living Values II Consultation at the Scarritt Bennett Center in Nashville, Tennessee, January 1993, 10-11. See also Anne Bathurst Gilson and Barbara A. Weaver, "Barriers among Us and Within Ourselves: Ethical Issues of Life in a Multicultural Society," *First, We Must Listen: Living in a Multicultural Society* (New York: Friendship Press, 1996), 95.
[295] Law, *The Bush Was Burning, But Not Consumed*, x.
[296] Foster, 52.
[297] Ibid., 53.
[298] Cox, 169.
[299] See Merton, "Blessed are the Meek."
[300] See, Thurman, *Footprints of a Dream*. Thurman shares the story of the founding and development of Fellowship Church throughout the book.
[301] Walter Brueggemann, "Biblical Authority" in *The Christian Century* (Chicago: The Christian Century, January 3-10, 2001), 16.
[302] Ewert Cousins, 2-3.
[303] Ibid., 3.
[304] Ibid.
[305] Ibid.

[306] Ibid.

[307] Brueggemann, *The Prophetic Imagination* (Minneapolis: Fortress Press, 1978), 80f.

[308] Thurman, *The Mood of Christmas*, 49.

[309] Langston Hughes, "I Dream a World," *The Collected Poems of Langston Hughes,* ed. Arnold Rampersad (New York; Vintage, 1994), 311.

[310] Thurman, *The Mood of Christmas*, 44.

[311] Ibid.

[312] Ibid, 49.

[313] Ibid.

[314] The views of Thurman and King with regard to *Agape* as a key to community-building are explicated at various places throughout their respective writings, but is clearly evident in Thurman, *Jesus and the Disinherited, and* King, *Strength to Love,* "Loving Your Enemies".

References and Bibliography

Primary Works by Howard Thurman

Thurman, Howard. *Apostles of Sensitiveness.* Boston:
American Unitarian Association, 1956.

Thurman, Howard. *The Centering Moment.* Richmond, IN:
Friends United Press, 1969.

Thurman, Howard. *The Creative Encounter: An Interpretation
of Religion and The Social Witness.* Richmond, IN: Friends
United Press, 1954.

Thurman, Howard. *Deep is the Hunger: Meditations for
Apostles of Sensitiveness.* New York: Harper and Brothers,
1951.

Thurman, Howard. *Deep River: An Interpretation of Negro
Spirituals.* Mills College, CA: Eucalyptus Press, 1945.

Thurman, Howard. *Deep River and the Negro Spiritual Speaks
of Life and Death.* Richmond, IN: Friends United Press, 1975.

Thurman, Howard. *Disciplines of the Spirit.* Richmond, IN:
Friends United Press, 1963.

Thurman, Howard. *Essential Writings.* Maryknoll, NY: Orbis
Press, 2006.

Thurman, Howard, ed. *The First Footprints – The Dawn of the
Idea of the Church for the Fellowship of All Peoples: Letters
Between Alfred Fisk and Howard Thurman.* San Francisco:
Lawton and Alfred Kennedy, 1975.

Thurman, Howard. *Footprints of a Dream: The Story of the Church for the Fellowship of All Peoples.* New York: Harper & Row, 1959.

Thurman, Howard. *For the Inward Journey: The Writings of Howard Thurman.* Richmond, IN: Friends United Press, 1984.

Thurman, Howard. *The Greatest of These.* Mills College, CA: Eucalyptus Press, 1944.

Thurman, Howard. *The Growing Edge.* Richmond, IN: Friends United Press, 1956.

Thurman, Howard. *The Inward Journey.* Richmond, IN: Friends United Press, 1971.

Thurman, Howard. *Jesus and the Disinherited.* Richmond, IN: Friends United Press,
        1969.
Thurman, Howard. *The Luminous Darkness.* Richmond, IN: Friends United Press, 1965.

Thurman, Howard. *Meditations for Apostles of Sensitiveness.* Mills College, CA: Eucalyptus Press, 1947.

Thurman, Howard. *Meditations of the Heart.* Richmond, IN: Friends United Press, 1953.

Thurman, Howard. *The Mood of Christmas.* Richmond, IN: Friends United Press, 1969.

Thurman, Howard. *Mysticism and the Experience of Love.* Wallingford, PA: Pendle Hill, 1961.

Thurman, Howard. *The Negro Spiritual Speaks of Life and Death.* New York: Harper & Row, 1947.

Thurman, Howard. *The Papers of Howard Thurman, vol. 1 (My People Need Me, June 1918-March 1936)*. Walter E. Fluker, senior editor. Columbia, SC: University of South Carolina Press, 2009.

Thurman, Howard. *The Papers of Howard Thurman, vol. 2 (Christian, Who Calls Me Christian?, April 1936-August 1943)*. Walter E. Fluker, senior editor. Columbia, SC: University of South Carolina Press, 2012.

Thurman, Howard. *The Papers of Howard Thurman, vol. 3 (The Bold Adventure, September 1943-May 1949)*. Walter E. Fluker, senior editor. Columbia, SC: University of South Carolina Press, 20157.

Thurman, Howard. *The Papers of Howard Thurman, vol. 4 (The Soundless Passion of a Single Mind, June1949-December 1963)*. Walter E. Fluker, senior editor. Columbia, SC: University of South Carolina Press, 2017.

Thurman, Howard. *The Papers of Howard Thurman, vol. 4 (The Wider Ministry, January 1963-April 1981)*. Walter E. Fluker, senior editor. Columbia, SC: University of South Carolina Press, 2019.

Thurman, Howard. *The Search for Common Ground: An Inquiry into the Basis of Man's Experience of Community*. Richmond, Indiana: Friends United Press, 1971.

Thurman, Howard. *Temptations of Jesus: Five Sermons*. Richmond, Indiana: Friends United Press, 1962.

Thurman, Howard, ed. *A Track to the Water's Edge: The Olive Schreiner Reader*. New York: Harper & Row, 1973.

Thurman, Howard. *With Head and Heart: The Autobiography of Howard Thurman.* New York: Harcourt, Brace and Jovanovich, 1979.

Secondary Works

Ansbro, John J. *Martin Luther King, Jr.: Nonviolent Strategies and Tactics for Social Change.* Maryknoll, NY: Orbis Books, 2000.

Baker-Fletcher, Garth. *Somebodyness: Martin Luther King, Jr. and the Theory of Dignity.* Minneapolis, MN: Fortress Press, 1993.

Baldwin, Lewis V. *There is a Balm in Gilead: The Cultural Roots of Martin Luther King, Jr.* Minneapolis: Fortress Press, 1993.

Barnes and Noble Books. *The Encyclopedia of Eastern Philosophy and Religion.* New York: Otto Wilhelm-Barth Verlag, 1986.

Bass, S. Jonathan Bass. *Blessed are the Peacemakers: Martin Luther King, Jr. Eight White Religious Leaders, and the Letter from Birmingham Jail.* Baton Rouge, LA: Louisiana State University Press, 2001.

Billingsley, Andrew. *Mighty Like a River: The Black Church and Social Reform.* Oxford, UK Oxford University Press, 1999.

Bondurant, Joan V. *Conquest of Violence: The Gandhian Philosophy of Conflict.* Princeton, NJ: Princeton University Press, 1958.

Bonhoeffer, Dietrich. *The Cost of Discipleship.* New York: Macmillan Publishing Company, 1963.

Bonhoeffer, Dietrich. *Christ the Center.* Trans. Edwin H. Robertson. New York: Harper Collins, 1960.

Bonhoeffer, Dietrich. *Life Together: The Classic Exploration of Faith in Community.* Trans. John Doberstein. New York: Harper Collins, 1954.

Bonhoeffer, Dietrich. *Meditations on the Cross.* Louisville: Westminster John Knox Press, 1996.

Bonhoeffer, Dietrich. *Who is Christ for Us?* Minneapolis: Fortress Press, 2002. Edited and Translated by Craig Nessan and Renate Wind.

Brueggemann, Walter. *Living Towards a Vision: Biblical Reflections on Shalom.* New York: United Church Press, 1976.

Brueggemann, Walter. *The Prophetic Imagination.* Minneapolis: Fortress Press, 1978.

Burrow, Rufus, Jr. *God and Human Dignity: The Personalism, Theology and Ethics of Martin Luther King, Kr.* Notre Dame, IN: University of Notre Dame Press, 2006.

Burrow, Rufus, Jr. *Personalism: A Critical Introduction.* St. Louis, MO: Chalice Press, 1999.

Caldwell, Gilbert H. *Race, Racism and Reconciliation.* Philadelphia: Simon, 1989.

Cauthen, Kenneth. *The Impact of American Religious Liberalism.* New York: Harper and Row, 1962.

Collyer, Charles E. and Ira G. Zepp, Jr. *Nonviolence Origins and Outcomes, second edition.* Victoria, BC, Canada: Trafford Publishing, 2006.

Cone, Cecil. *The Identity Crisis in Black Theology.* Nashville: AMEC Press, 1975.

Cone, James H. *A Black Theology of Liberation.* New York: J. B. Lippincott Co, 1970.

Cone, James H. *Black Theology and Black Power.* New York: Harper & Row, 1969.

Cone, James H. *The Cross and the Lynching Tree.* New York: Orbis Books, 2015.

Cone, James H. *For My People: Black Theology and the Black Church.* Maryknoll, NY: Orbis Books, 1984.

Cone, James H. *God of the Oppressed.* New York: Seabury Press, 1975.

Cone, James H. *The Spirituals and the Blues.* Maryknoll, NY: Orbis, 1972.

Cousins, Ewert H. *Christ of the 21st Century.* New York: Continuum, 1998.

Cox, Harvey. *Many Mansions: A Christian's Encounter with Other Faiths.* Boston: Beacon Press, 1988.

Cross, George. *What is Christianity?- A Study of Rival Interpretations.* Chicago: University of Chicago Press, 1918.

Cross, George. *Christian Salvation: A Modern Interpretation.* Chicago: University of Chicago Press, 1925.

Dalton, Harlan. *Racial Healing: Confronting the Fear Between Blacks and Whites.* New York: Anchor Books, 1995.

Dash, Michael I. N., Jonathan Jackson and Stephen C. Rasor. *Hidden Wholeness: An African American Spirituality for Individuals and Communities.* Cleveland, OH: United Church Press, 1997.

Davies, Susan E. and Sister Paul Teresa Hennessee, S.A. *Ending Racism in the Church.* Cleveland, OH: United Church Press, 1998.

DeYoung, Curtis Paul. *Coming Together: The Bible's Message in an Age of Diversity.* Valley Forge, PA: Judson Press, 1995.

Dixon, Quinton and Peter Eisenstadt. *Visions of Better World: Howard Thurman's Pilgrimage to India and the Origins of African American Nonviolence.* Boston: Beacon Press, 2011.

Dorrien, Gary. *Breaking White Supremacy: Martin Luther King, Jr. and the Black Social Gospel.* New Haven, Ct: Yale University Press, 2018.

Douglas, Kelly Brown. *Stand Your Ground: Black Bodies and the Justice of God.* Maryknoll, NY: Orbis Press, 2015.

DuBois, W. E. B. *The Souls of Black Folk.* Chicago: A. C. McClurg & Co., 1903.

Dyson, Michael Eric. *Reflecting Black: African-American Cultural Criticism.* Minneapolis: University of Minnesota Press, 1993.

Dyson, Michael Eric. *Tears We Cannot Stop: A Sermon to White America.* New York: McMillan, 2017.

Egan, Eileen. *Peace Be With You: Justified Warfare or the Way of Nonviolence.* Maryknoll, NY: Orbis, 1999.

Erikson, Erik H. *Gandhi's Truth: On the Origins of Militant Nonviolence.* New York: W. W. Norton and Company, 1969.

Emerson, Michael and Christian Smith. *Divided by Faith: Evangelical Religion and the Problem of Race.* Oxford, UK: Oxford University Press, 2000.

Epperly, Bruce. *The Works of Christmas; The 12 Days of Christmas with Howard Thurman.* Vestal, NY: Anamcharabooks, 2017.

Evans, James H. *We Have Been Believers: An African-American Systematic Theology.* Minneapolis: Fortress Press, 1992.

Featherstone, Mike. *Undoing Culture: Globalization, Postmodernism and Identity.* London, UK: SAGE Publications, 1995.

Felder, Cain Hope. *Troubling Biblical Waters: Race, Class and Family.* Maryknoll, NY: Orbis, 1989.

Fischer, Louis. *Gandhi: His Life and Message for the World.* New York: Mentor Books, 1954.

Fisher, Louis, ed. *The Essential Gandhi: An Anthology of His Writings on His Life, Work and Ideas.* New York: Vintage Books, 1962.

Fitzgerald, Kelley, ed. *Racism: The Church's Unfinished Agenda – A Journal of the National United Methodist Convocation on Racism.* Washington, DC: The United Methodist Church, General Commission on Religion and Race, 1987.

Fluker, Walter Earl, ed. *The Stones the Builders Rejected: The Development of Ethical Leadership from the Black Church Tradition.* Harrisburg, PA: Trinity Press International, 1998.

Fluker, Walter Earl. *They Looked For a City: A Comparative Analysis of the Ideal of Community in the Thought of Howard Thurman and Martin Luther King, Jr.* New York: University Press of America, 1989.

Fluker, Walter Earl and Catherine Tumber, eds. *A Strange Freedom: The Best of Howard Thurman on Religious Experience and Public Life.* Boston: Beacon Books, 1998.

Foster, Charles R. *Embracing Diversity.* Washington, DC: Alban Institute, 1997.

Foster, Charles R. and Theodore Brelsford. *We are the Church Together: Cultural Diversity in Congregational Life.* Valley Forge, PA: Trinity Press International, 1996.

Fong, Bruce W. *Racial Equality in the Church: A Critique of the Homogeneous Unit Principle in Light of a Practical Theology Perspective.* Lanham, MD: University Press of America, 1996.

Fox, Matthew. *Creation Spirituality: Liberating Gifts for The Peoples of the Earth.* New York: HarperCollins, 1991.

Fox, Matthew. *A Spirituality Named Compassion and the Healing of the Global Village, Humpty Dumpty and Us.* Minneapolis: Winston Press, 1979.

Frankl, Victor. *Man's Search for Meaning.* Boston, MS: Beacon Press, 1959.

Franklin, John Hope and Alfred A. Moss, Jr. *From Slavery to Freedom: A History of African Americans.* New York: McGraw Hill, 1994.

Franklin, Robert M. *Another Day's Journey: Black Church Confronting the American Crisis.* Minneapolis: Fortress Press, 1997.

Franklin, Robert M. *Liberating Visions: Human Fulfillment and Social Justice in African American Thought.* Minneapolis: Fortress Press, 1990.

Frazier, E. Franklin. *The Negro Church in America.* New York: Schocken Books, 1963.

Fulop, Timothy E. and Albert J. Raboteau, eds. *African-American Religion: Interpretive Essays in History and Culture.* New York: Routledge, 1997.

Gandhi, Mohandas K. *Autobiography: The Story of My Experiments with Truth.* New York: Dover Publications, 1983.

Gandhi, Mohandas K. *Peace: The Words and Inspiration of Mahatma Gandhi.* Boulder, Colorado: Blue Mountain Press, 2007.

Gandhi, Mohandas K. *Non-violence in Peace and War,* Vol. 1. Ahmedabad: Navajivan Publishing House, 1942.

Gandhi, Mohandas K. *The Way to God.* Berkley, CA: Berkley Hills Books, 1999.

Gaustad, Edwin S., ed. *A Documentary History of Religion in America, Since 1865.* Grand Rapids, MI: Eerdmans Publishing, 1993.

Goldberg, David Theo, ed. *Multiculturalism: A Critical Reader.* Oxford, UK: Blackwell, 1994.

Gowler, David B. and Kipton E. Jenson, eds. *Howard Thurman: Sermons on the Parables.* Maryknoll, NY: Orbis Books, 2018.

Griggs, Lewis Brown and Lente-Louise Louw. *Valuing Diversity: New Tools for a New Reality.* New York: McGraw Hill, 1995.

Gutierrez, Gustavo. *On Job: God-Talk and the Suffering of the Innocent.* Maryknoll, NY: Orbis Books, 1985.

Gutierrez, Gustavo. *A Theology of Liberation.* Maryknoll: NY: Orbis Books, 1971.

Gutierrez, Gustavo. *We Drink from Our Own Wells: The Spiritual Journey of a People.* Maryknoll, NY: Orbis Books, 1984.

Hall, Edward T. *Beyond Culture.* New York: Doubleday, 1976.

Hall, Edward T. *The Dance of Life.* New York: Doubleday, 1983.

Hall, Edward T. *The Hidden Dimension.* New York: Doubleday, 1966.

Hall, Edward T. *The Silent Language.* New York: Doubleday, 1973.

Harding, Vincent. *Hope and History: Why We Must Share the Story of the Movement.* Maryknoll: New York: Orbis, 1990.

Haring, Bernard. *The Healing Power of Peace and Non-violence.* New York: Paulist Press, 1986.

Hendricks, Obery M. *The Politics of Jesus: Rediscovering the Revolutionary Nature of Jesus' Teachings and How They Have Been Corrupted.* New York: Doubleday, 2006.

Heschel, Abraham Joshua. *Man is Not Alone: A Philosophy of Religion.* New York: Farrar, Straus and Giroux, 1951.

Heschel, Susannah, ed. *Moral Grandeur and Spiritual Audacity.* New York: Farrar, Straus and Giroux, 1997.

Hopkins, Dwight N. *Introducing to Black Theology of Liberation.* Maryknoll: NY:Orbis, 1999.

Hopkins, Dwight N. *Shoes That Fit Our Feet: Sources for a Constructive Black Theology.* Maryknoll, NY: Orbis, 1993.

Hunt, C. Anthony. "The Search for Peaceful Community: A Comparative Analysis of the Thinking of Howard Thurman and Martin Luther King, Jr." Ph.D. Dissertation. Graduate Theological Foundation, Donaldson, IN, 2001.

Hunt, C. Anthony. *Blessed are the Peacemakers: A Theological Analysis of the Thought of Howard Thurman and Martin Luther King, Jr.* Lima, OH: Wyndham Hall Press, 2005.

Hunt, C. Anthony. *And Yet the Melody Lingers: Essays, Sermons and Prayers on Religion and Race.* Lima, OH: Wyndham Hall Press, 2006.

Hunt, C. Anthony. *My Hope is Built: Essays, Sermons and Prayers on Religion and Race, vol. 2.* Lima, OH: Wyndham Hall Press, 2011.

Hunt, C. Anthony. *Keep Looking Up: Sermons on the Psalms.* Lima, OH: Wyndham Hall Press, 2016.

Hunt, C. Anthony. *Stones of Hope: Essays, Sermons and Prayers on Religion and Race, vol. 3.* Lima, OH: Wyndham Hall Press, 2018.

Hunt, C. Anthony. *Upon the Rock: A Model for Ministry with Black Families.* Lima, OH: Wyndham Hall Press, 2001.

Ivory, Luther D. *Toward a Theology of Radical Involvement: The Theological Legacy of Martin Luther King, Jr.* Nashville, TN: Abingdon, 1997.

Jesudasan, Ignatius. *A Gandhian Theology of Liberation.* Maryknoll, NY: Orbis, 1984.

James, William. *The Varieties of Religious Experience: A Study of Human Nature – Being the Gifford Lectures on Natural Religion Delivered at Edinburgh in 1901-1902.* New York: The Modern Library, 1999.

Johnson, Alonzo. *Good News for the Disinherited: Howard Thurman on Jesus of Nazareth and Human Liberation.* New York: University Press of America, 1997.

Johnson, Elizabeth. *Quest for the Living God: Mapping Frontiers in the Theology of God.* New York: Bloomsbury, 2007.

Johnson, Elizabeth. *She Who Is: The Mystery of God in Feminist Theological Discourse.* New York: The Crossroad Publishing Company, 1992.

Jones, Cheslyn, Jeffrey Wainwright and Edward Yarnold, eds. *The Study of Spirituality.* Oxford, UK: Oxford University Press, 1986.

Jones, E. Stanley. *Gandhi: Portrayal of a Friend.* Nashville: Abingdon, 1948.

Jones, William R. *Is God a White Racist: A Preamble to Black Theology.* Boston: Beacon Books, 1973.

Jordan, Clarence. *The Cotton Patch Version of Matthew and John.* New York: Association Press, 1970.

Jordan, Clarence. *Sermon on the Mount.* Valley Forge, PA: Judson Press, 1952.

Kapur, Sudarshan. *Raising Up a Prophet: The African American Encounter with Gandhi.* Boston: Beacon Press, 1992.

Kelsey, George D. *Racism and the Christian Understanding of Man.* Eugene, OR: Wipf an Stock Publishers, 1965.

King, Martin Luther, Jr. "A Comparison of the Conceptions of God in the Thinking of Paul Tillich and Henry Nelson Wieman." Ph.D. Dissertation. Boston, MA: Boston University, 1955.

King, Martin Luther, Jr. *Strength to Love.* New York: Harper & Row, 1963.

King, Martin Luther, Jr. *Stride Toward Freedom: The Montgomery Story.* New York: Harper & Row, 1958.

King, Martin Luther, Jr. *Where Do We Go From Here: Chaos or Community?* New York: Harper & Row, 1967.

King, Martin Luther, Jr. *Why We Can't Wait.* New York: HarperCollins, 1963.

King, Preston and Walter E. Fluker, eds. *Black Leaders and Ideologies in the South: Resistance and Nonviolence,* London, UK: Taylor and Francis Ltd. *Critical Review of International Social and Political Philosophy,* Winter 2004, special issue.

King, Preston and Walter E. Fluker, eds. *Black Leaders and Ideologies in the South: Resistance and Nonviolence.* New York: Routledge, 2005.

Kohls, L. Robert. *Developing Intercultural Awareness.* Yarmouth, ME: Intercultural Press, 1994.

Law, Eric H. F. *The Bush Was Burning, But Not Consumed.* St. Louis, MO: Chalice Press, 1996.

Law, Eric H. F. *Inclusion: Making Room for Grace.* St. Louis, MO: Chalice Press, 2000.

Law, Eric H. F. *The Wolf Shall Dwell with the Lamb: A Spirituality for Leadership in a Multicultural Community.* St. Louis, MO: Chalice Press, 1993.

Lebacqz, Karen. *Justice in an Unjust World.* Minneapolis: Augsburg Publishing House, 1987.

Lincoln, C. Eric. *The Black Church Since Frazier.* New York: Schocken Books, 1974.

Lincoln, C. Eric. *Coming Through the Fire: Surviving Race and Place in America.* Durham, NC: Duke University Press, 1996.

Lincoln, C. Eric. *Martin Luther King: A Profile.* New York: Hill & Wang, 1970.

Lincoln, C. Eric. *Race, Religion and the Continuing American Dilemma.* New York: Hill & Wang, 1984.

Lincoln, C. Eric and Lawrence Mamiya. *The Black Church in the African-American Experience.* Durham, NC: Duke University Press, 1990.

Lingenfelter, Sherwood G. *Ministering Cross-Culturally: An Incarnational Model for Personal Relationships.* Grand Rapids, MI: Baker Books House, 1986.

Locke, Don C. *Increasing Multicultural Understanding.* Thousand Oaks, CA; Sage Publications, 1992.

Long, Edward, L. *Peace Thinking in a Warring World: An Urgent Call for a New Approach to Peace.* Philadelphia: Westminster Press, 1983.

Lovin, Robin, et al. *Creating a New Community: God's People Overcoming Racism.* Nashville: Graded Press, 1989.

Lyght, Ernest S. *The Religious and Philosophical Foundations in the Thought of Martin Luther King, Jr.* New York: Vantage Press, 1972.

Lynd, Straughton and Alice Lynd, eds. *Nonviolence in America: A Documentary History.* Maryknoll, NY: Orbis, 1995.

Macquarrie, John. *Christian Unity and Christian Diversity.* London: SCM Press, 1975.

Makechnie, George K. *Howard Thurman: His Enduring Dream.* Boston, MA: The Howard University Center, 1988.

Marable, Manning. *Race, Reform, and Rebellion: The Second Reconstruction in Black America: Problems in Race, Political Economy, and Society.* Boston: South End Press, 1983.

Marsh, Charles. *The Beloved Community: How Faith Shapes Social Justice from the Civil Rights Movement.* New York: Basic Books, 2005.

Marty, Martin E. *Pilgrims in Their Own Land: 500 Years of Religion in America.* New York: Penguin Books, 1984.

Mathabane, Mark. *Kaffir Boy: The True Story of a Black Youth's Coming of Age in Apartheid South Africa.* New York: Plume, 1986.

Matthews, James K. *The Matchless Weapon: Satyagraha.* Bombay, India: Bharatiya Vidya Bhavan, 1989.

Matsuoka, Fumitaka. *The Color of Faith: Building Community in a Multicultural Society.* Cleveland, OH: United Church Press, 1998.

Mbiti, John. *African Religions and Philosophy.* New York: Anchor Books, 1970.

McClain, William B. *Black People in the United Methodist Church: Whither Thou Goest?* Nashville: Abingdon, 1990.

McClain, William B. *Travelling Light.* New York: Friendship Press, 1981.

McMickle, Marvin. *Where Have All the Prophets Gone?* Cleveland, OH: Pilgrim Press, 2006.

Meeks, Wayne A. *The Writings of St. Paul.* New York: Norton, 1978.

Merton, Thomas. *Contemplation in a World of Action.* Notre Dame, IN: University of Notre Dame Press, 1998.

Merton, Thomas. *Faith and Violence: Christian Teaching and Christian Practice.* Notre Dame, IN: University of Notre Dame Press, 1968.

Merton, Thomas. *Gandhi on Nonviolence.* New York: New Directions, 1964.

Merton, Thomas. *The Nonviolent Alternative (*Revised edition of *Thomas Merton on Peace).* New York: Farrar, Straus and Giroux, 1980.

Metzger, Bruce M. and Roland E. Murphy, eds. *The New Oxford Annotated Bible with the Apocryphl /*

Deuterocanonical Books (New Revised Standard Version). New York: Oxford University Press, 1991.

Metzger, Bruce M. and Michael D. Coogan, eds. *The Oxford Companion to the Bible.* New York: Oxford University Press, 1993.

Mitchell, Henry and Nicholas Cooper Lewter. *Soul Theology; The Heart of American Black Culture.* New York: Harper and Row, 1986.

Mitchell, Mozella Gordon. "The Dynamics of Howard Thurman's Relationship to Literature and Theology." Ph.D. Dissertation. Atlanta: Emory University, 1983.

Mitchell, Mozella Gordon. *Spiritual Dynamics of Howard Thurman's Theology.* Bristol, IN: Wyndham Hall Press, 1985.

Moltmann, Jürgen. *A Theology of Hope.* Minneapolis, MN: Fortress, 1993.

Moses, Greg. *Revolution of Conscience: Martin Luther King, Jr. and the Philosophy of Nonviolence.* New York: Guilford Press, 1997.

Moyd, Olin P. *Redemption in Black Theology.* Valley Forge, PA: Judson Press, 1979.

Moyd, Olin P. *Sacred Art: Preaching and Theology in the African American Tradition.* Valley Forge, PA: Judson Press, 1995.

Myrdal, Gunnar. *An American Dilemma: The Negro Problem and Modern Democracy.* New York: Harper and Row, 1944.

Niebuhr, H. Richard. *Christ and Culture.* New York: Harper & Row, 1951.

Niebuhr, Reinhold. *Moral Man and Immoral Society.* New York: Scribner, 1933.

Nouwen, Henri J. M. *The Path of Peace.* New York: Crossroad, 1995.

Nunez, Emilio A., translated by Paul E. Sywulka. *Liberation Theology.* Chicago: Moody Press, 1995.

Obama, Barack. *The Audacity of Hope: Thoughts on Reclaiming the American Dream.* New York: Three Rivers Press, 2006.

Panikkar, Raimundo. *The Unknown Christ in Hinduism.* Revised edition. Maryknoll, NY: Orbis Books, 1982.

Parekh, Bhikhu. *Gandhi: A Very Short Introduction.* Oxford, UK: University of Oxford Press, 1997.

Park, Andrew Sung. *Racial Conflict and Healing: An Asian-American Theological Perspective.* New York: Orbis, 1996.

Paris, Peter J. *Black Religious Leaders: Conflict and Unity.* Louisville: Westminster/John Knox Press, 1991.

Paris, Peter J. *The Social Teaching of the Black Churches.* Philadelphia: Fortress Press, 1985.

Paris, Peter J. *The Spirituality of African Peoples: The Search for a Common Moral Discourse.* Minneapolis: Fortress Press, 1995.

Paston, Amy. *Gandhi: A Photographic Story of a Life.* London: D. K. Publishing, 2006.

Peck, M. Scott. *The Different Drum: Community Making and Peace: A Spiritual Journey Toward Self-Acceptance, True Belonging and New Hope for the World.* New York: Touchstone Books, 1987.

Peck, M. Scott. *People of the Lie: The Hope for Healing Human Evil.* New York: Simon & Schuster, 1983.

Pollard, Alton B., III. *Mysticism and Social Change: The Social Witness of Howard Thurman.* New York: Lang, 1992.

Raboteau, Albert. *Canaan Land: A Religious History of African Americans.* Oxford, UK; Oxford University Press, 2001.

Rauschenbusch, Walter. *Christianity and the Social Crisis.* New York; Harper & Row, 1907.

Rauschenbusch, Walter. *A Theology of the Social Gospel.* Louisville, KY: Westminster John Knox Press. 1954.

Recinos, Harold J. *Jesus Weeps: Global Encounters on Our Doorstep.* Nashville: Abingdon, 1992.

Recinos, Harold J. *Who Comes in the Name of the Lord: Jesus at the Margins.* Nashville: Abingdon, 1997.

Reid, Stephen Breck. *Listening In: A Multicultural Reading of the Psalms.* Nashville: Abingdon, 1997.

Roberts, J. Deotis. *Africentric Christianity: A Theological Appraisal for Ministry.* Valley Forge, PA: Judson Press, 2000.

Roberts, J. Deotis. *Liberation and Reconciliation: A Black Theology.* New York: Orbis, 1994.

Roberts, J. Deotis. *The Prophethood of Black Believers: An African American Political Theology for Ministry.* Louisville, KY: Westminster John Knox Press, 1994.

Schaper, Donna, ed. *40-Day Journey with Howard Thurman.* Minneapolis, MN: Augsburg Books, 2009.

Sernett, Milton C., ed. *Afro-American Religious History: A Documentary Witness.* Durham, NC: Duke University Press, 1985.

Shannon, William H. *Seeds of Peace: Contemplation and Non-Violence.* New York: Crossroad Publishing, 1996.

Smith, Huston. *The World's Religions.* New York: Harper Collins, 1991.

Smith, Kenneth and Ira Zepp, Jr. *Search for the Beloved Community.* Valley Forge, PA: Judson Press, 1974.

Smith, Luther E., Jr. *Howard Thurman: The Mystic as Prophet.* Richmond, Indiana: Friends United Press, 1991.

Sobrino, Jon. *Spirituality of Liberation: Toward Political Holiness.* Maryknoll: Orbis Books, 1988.

Solle, Dorothy. *Suffering.* Philadelphia: Fortress Press, 1975

Solle, Dorothee. *Thinking About God: An Introduction to Theology.* Philadelphia: Trinity Press, 1990.

Sowell, Thomas S. *Race and Culture: A World View.* New York: Basic Books, 1994.

Spencer, Jon Michael. *Protest and Praise: Sacred Music of Black Religion.* Minneapolis: Fortress Press, 1990.

Stassen, Glen H. *Just Peacemaking: Transforming Initiatives for Justice and Peace.* Louisville, KY: Westminster john Knox Press, 1992.

Steele, Shelby. *The Content of Our Character: A New Vision for Race in America.* New York: Harper Perennial, 1990.

Stevenson, Bryan. *Just Mercy: A Story of Justice and Redemption.* New York: Penguin Random House. 2014.

Stewart, Carlyle Fielding, III. "A Comparative Analysis of Theological-Ontological and Ethical Method in the Theologies of James H. Cone and Howard Thurman." Ph.D. Dissertation. Evanston, IL: Northwestern University, 1982.

Stewart, Carlyle Fielding, III. *God, Being and Liberation: A Comparative Analysis of the Theologies of James Cone and Howard Thurman.* Lanham, MD: University Press, 1989.

Stewart, Carlyle Fielding, III. *Soul Survivors: An African American Spirituality.* Louisville, KY: Westminster John Knox, 1997.

Stewart, Edward C. and Milton J. Bennett. *American Cultural Patterns: A Cross-Cultural Persepective.* Yarmouth, ME, Intercultural Press, 1991.

Storti, Craig. *Cross-Cultural Dialogues.* Yarmouth, ME: Intercultural Press, 1994.

Storti, Craig. *The Art of Crossing Cultures.* Yarmouth, ME: Intercultural Press, 1989.

Sutherland, Arthur. *I was a Stranger: A Christian Theology of Hospitality.* Nashville: Abingdon Press, 2006.

Thomas, James S. *Methodism's Racial Dilemma: The Story of the Central Jurisdiction.* Nashville: Abingdon, 1992.

Thompson, Marjorie. *Soul Feast: An Invitation to the Christian Spiritual Life.* Louisville, KY: Westminster John Knox Press, 1995.

Thoreau, Henry David. *Civil Disobedience and Other Essays.* New York: Dover Publications, 1993.

Tillich, Paul. *The Courage to Be.* New Haven, CT: Yale University Press, 1952.

Tillich, Paul. *Love, Power, and Justice.* London: Oxford University Press, 1954.

Tillich, Paul. *Theology of Peace.* Louisville: Westminster/John Knox, 1990.

Townes, Emily M., ed. *A Troubling in My Soul: Womanist Perspectives on Evil and Suffering.* New York: Orbis, 1993.

Townes, Emily M., ed. *Embracing the Spirit: Womanist Perspectives on Hope, Salvation and Transformation.* New York: Orbis, 1997.

Townes, Emily M. *In a Blaze of Glory: Womanist Spirituality As Social Witness.* Abingdon, 1995.

Tutu, Desmond. *No Future Without Forgiveness.* New York: Doubleday, 1999.

Volf, Miroslav. *Exclusion or Embrace: A Theological Exploration of Identity, Otherness, and Reconciliation.* Nashville: Abingdon, 1996.

Volf, Miroslav. *A Public Faith: How Followers of Christ Should Serve the Common Good.* Grand Rapids, MI: Brazos Press, 2011.

Walker, Wyatt T. *Somebody's Calling My Name: Black Sacred Music and Social Change.* Valley Forge, PA: Judson Press, 1992.

Wallis, Jim. *America's Original Sin: Racism, White Privilege and the Bridge to a New America.* Grand Rapids, MI: Brazos Press, 2017.

Wallis, Jim. *God's Politics: Why the Right Gets it Wrong and the Left Doesn't Get It.* San Francisco, CA: Harper, 2005.

Wallis, Jim. *On God's Side: What Religion Forgets and Politics Hasn't Learned about Serving the Common Good.* Grand Rapids, MI: Brazos Press, 2013.

Wallis, Jim. *The Soul of Politics: Beyond the "Religious Right" and "Secular Left."* San Diego, CA: Harcourt Brace and Company, 1994.

Wallis, Jim. *The (Un) Common Good: How the Gospel Brings Hope to the World Divided.* Grand Rapids, MI: Brazos Press, 2013..

Ward, Graham, ed. *The Postmodern God: A Theological Reader.* Oxford, UK: Blackwell Publishers, 1997.

Washington, James Melvin. *Frustrated Fellowships: The Black Baptist Quest for Social Power.* Macon: Mercer University Press, 1986.

Washington, James Melvin, ed. *A Testament of Hope: The Essential Writings and Speeches of Martin Luther King, Jr.* New York: Harper Collins, 1986.

Washington, Raleigh and Glen Kehrein. *Breaking Down Walls: A Model for Reconciliation in an Age of Racial Strife.* Chicago: Moody Press, 1993.

Watley, William D. *Roots of Resistance.* Valley Forge, PA: Judson Press, 1985.

West, Cornel. *Keeping Faith: Philosophy and Race in America.* New York: Routledge, 1993.

West, Cornel. *Hope on a Tightrope.* New York: Smiley Books, 2008.

West, Cornel. *Prophesy Deliverance! An Afro-American Revolutionary Christianity.* Philadelphia: Westminster Press, 1982.

West, Cornel. *Prophetic Fragments: Illuminations of the Crisis in American Religion and Culture.* Grand Rapids, MI: Eerdmans, 1988.

West, Cornel. *Prophetic Reflections: Notes on Race and Power in America.* Philadelphia: Westminster Press, 1982.

West, Cornel. *Race Matters.* Boston: Beacon Press, 1993.

West, Russell W. "That His People May be One: An Interpretive Analysis of the Pentecostal Leadership's Quest of Racial Unity." Ph.D. Dissertation. Virginia Beach, VA: Regent University, 1998.

Williams, Reggie L. *Bonhoeffer's Black Jesus: Harlem Renaissance Theology and an Ethic of Resistance.* Waco, TX: Baylor University Press, 2014.

Wilmore, Gayraud. *Black Religion and Black Radicalism.* Maryknoll, NY: Orbis Books, 1989.

Wilson, William Julius. *The Bridge Over the Racial Divide: Rising Inequality and Coalition Politics.* Berkley, CA: University of California Press, 1999.

Wilson, William Julius. *The Declining Significance of Race: Blacks and Changing American Institutions.* Chicago: University of Chicago Press, 1978.

Wilson, William Julius. *Power, Racism and Privilege: Race Relations in Theoretical and Sociological Perspectives.* New York: The Free Press, 1973.

Wimberly, Anne Streaty and Edward Wimberly. *Language of Hospitality: Intercultural Relations in the Household of God.* Nashville: Cokesbury, 1989.

Wink, Walter, ed. *Peace is the Way: Writings on Nonviolence from the Fellowship of Reconciliation.* New York: Orbis Books, 2000.

Wiseman, Richard L. and Jolene Koester. *Intercultural Communication Competence.* Newbury Park, CA: Sage, 1993.

Wogaman, J. Philip. *Christian Moral Judgment.* Louisville: Westminster/John Knox Press, 1989.

Wogaman, J. Philip. *Christian Perspectives on Politics.* Louisville, KY: Westminster John Knox Press, 2000.

Wolpert, Stanley. *Gandhi's Passion: The Life and Legacy of Mahatma Gandhi.* Oxford, UK: Oxford university Press, 2001.

Wolterstorff, Nicholas. *Until Justice and Peace Embrace.* Grand Rapids, MI: Eerdmans,1983.

Yates, Elizabeth. *Howard Thurman: Portrait of a Practical Dreamer.* New York: John Day, 1964.

Young, Josiah U. *Black and African Theologies: Siblings or Distant Cousins.* Maryknoll, NY: Orbis Books, 1990.

Young, Josiah U. *No Difference in the Fare: Dietrich Bonhoeffer and the Problem of Racism.* Grand Rapids, MI: Eerdmans, 1998.

Articles

Bennett, Lerone, Jr. "Eulogy of Howard Thurman: Tributes to Genius," *The African American Pulpit*. Valley Forge, PA: Judson, Winter 2001.

Bennet, Milton J. "A Developmental Approach to Training for Intercultural Sensitivity," *Theories and Methods in Cross-Cultural Orientation.* ed. Judith N. Martin, International Journal of Intercultural Relations, Vol. 5, No. 2. New York: Persimmon Press, 1986.

Bennett, Milton J. "Toward Ethnorelativism: A Developmental Model of Intercultural Sensitivity," *Cross-Cultural Orientation.* ed. R. Michael Paige. Lanham, MD: University Press of America, 1986.

Booth, Newell S. "An Approach to African Religion," *African Religions: A Symposium.* ed. Newell S. Booth. New York: NOK Publishers, 1977.

Cone, James "Theology's Great Sin: Silence in the Face of White Supremacy" in Black Theology, 2:2 (Maryknoll, NY: Orbis Books, 2004)

Dear, John. "The Experiments of Gandhi," *Fellowship.* New York: The Fellowship of Reconciliation, January/February, 1988.

Denard, Carolyn C. "Retrieving and Reappropriating the Values of the Black Church Tradition Through Written Narratives," *The Stones that the Builders Rejected.* ed. Walter E. Fluker. Harrisburg, PA: Trinity Press International, 1998.

Fluker, Walter. "Dangerous Memories and Redemptive Possibilities: Reflections on the Life and Work of Howard Thurman" in *Black Leaders and Ideologies in the South: Resistance and Nonviolence*, edited by Preston King and Walter E. Fluker, New York: Routledge, 2005, pp. 147-176.

Galilea, Segundo. "Liberation as an Encounter with Politics and Contemplation," *The Mystical Dimension of the Christian Faith.*

Gandhi, Mohandas K. "Nonviolence – The Greatest Force," *The World Tomorrow,* October, 1926.

Gandhi, Rajmohan. "Gandhi's Unfulfilled Legacy: Prospects for Reconciliation in Racial/Ethnic Conflict" (1995 Cynthia Wedel Lecture). Washington, DC: Church's Center for Theology and Public Policy, Wesley Theological Seminary, April 27, 1995.

Goodwin, Mary E. "Racial Roots and Religion: An Interview with Howard Thurman," *The Christian Century.* Chicago: The Christian Century, 9 May 1973.

Harding, Vincent. "Dangerous Spirituality." Sojourners Magazine, January-February 1999 (Vol. 28, No. 1, pp. 28-31).

Hunt, C. Anthony. *The Beloved Community Toolkit.* (Self-publisher, 2018).

Hunt, C. Anthony . "Martin Luther King, Jr. and the Quest for Beloved Community" in the *American Baptist Quarterly.* Atlanta, Georgia: American Baptist Historical Society, Spring 2018.

Hunt, C. Anthony . "Martin Luther King, Jr.: Resistance, Non-Violence and Community" in *Black Leaders and Ideologies in the South: Resistance and Nonviolence*, edited by Preston King and Walter E. Fluker, New York: Routledge, 2005, pp. 227-251.

Hunt, C. Anthony. "Martin Luther King, Jr.: Resistance, Non-Violence and Community" in *Black Leaders and Ideologies in the South: Resistance and Nonviolence*, edited by Preston King and Walter E. Fluker, London, UK: Taylor and Francis

Ltd., Winter 2004, special issue - *Critical Review of International Social and Political Philosophy* , vol. 7, no.4, pp. 227-251.

Hunt, C. Anthony. "Howard Thurman and the Identity of Jesus," *FOUNDATION THEOLOGY 2004,* Graduate Theological Foundation, South Bend, IN, 2004 (Faculty Publication Series), pp. 73-93.

Jensen, Kipton and Preston King, "Beloved Community: Martin Luther King, Howard Thurman and Josiah Royce". Atlanta: Morehouse Faculty Publication, #23, 2017.

King, Martin Luther, Jr. "Pilgrimage to Nonviolence," in *A Testament of Hope: The Essential Writings and Speeches of Martin Luther King, Jr.* James Melvin Washington, ed. New York: Harper Collins, 1986.

Maguire, Mairead Corrigan. "Gandhi and the Ancient Wisdom of Nonviolence," *Fellowship.* New York: Fellowship for Reconciliation, June 1988.

Roberts, J. Deotis. "Gandhi and King: On Conflict Resolution," in *Shalom Papers: A Journal of Theology and Public Policy,* ed. Victoria J. Barnett. Washington, DC: Church's Center for Theology and Public Policy, Vol. 11, No. 2, Spring 2000.

Thurman, Howard. "Mysticism and Social Action," *Eden Theological Seminary Bulletin IV,* St. Louis, Missouri, Spring, 1939.

Thurman, Howard. "The Will to Segregate," *Fellowship.* New York: The Fellowship of Reconciliation, August, 1943.

Williams, Robert C. "Worship and Anti-Structure in Thurman's Vision of the Sacred," *The Journal of the Interdenominational Theological Center,* Melva Costen and Darius Swann, eds. Atlanta, Georgia: Interdenominational Theological Center, Volume XIV, Fall 1986-Spring 1987.

ABOUT THE AUTHOR

C. ANTHONY HUNT, D.MIN., PH.D.

A native of Washington D.C., Rev. Dr. C. Anthony Hunt currently serves as Senior Pastor of Epworth Chapel United Methodist Church in Baltimore, MD, and as Professor of Systematic, Moral and Practical Theology and Permanent Dunning Distinguished Lecturer at the Ecumenical Institute of Theology, St. Mary's Seminary and University in Baltimore. He also teaches at Wesley Theological Seminary in Washington, DC, United Theological Seminary in Dayton, OH and the Graduate Theological Foundation in Mishawaka, IN, where he is a Faculty Fellow and E. Franklin Frazier Professor of African-American Studies.

A graduate of the University of Maryland, he holds advanced degrees from Troy State University, Wesley Theological Seminary and the Graduate Theological Foundation. Additionally, he has completed post-graduate studies at the Center of Theological Inquiry, Princeton NJ; the University of Oxford, UK;; St. Mary's Seminary and University, Baltimore, MD; and the Institute of Certified Professional Managers, James Madison University, Harrisonburg, Va.

He is the author of eight other books including: *Stones of Hope: Essays, Sermons and Prayers on Religion and Race, vol.3* (2017), *Keep Looking Up: Sermons on the Psalms*

(2016), and *Blessed are the Peacemakers: A Theological Analysis of the Thought of Howard Thurman and Martin Luther King, Jr.* (2005), and over 150 articles and chapters on matters pertaining to religion and society. He is also an active blogger at www.newurbanministry.blogspot.com.

www.ingramcontent.com/pod-product-compliance
Lightning Source LLC
Chambersburg PA
CBHW030827090426
42737CB00009B/904